Modern China

A Captivating Guide to Modern Chinese History

Free Bonus from Captivating History (Available for a Limited time)

Hi History Lovers!

Now you have a chance to join our exclusive history list so you can get your first history ebook for free as well as discounts and a potential to get more history books for free! Simply visit the link below to join.

Captivatinghistory.com/ebook

Also, make sure to follow us on Facebook, Twitter and Youtube by searching for Captivating History.

Table of Contents

Introduction

With a population of over 1.4 billion people and occupying over 9.5 million square kilometers of land in Asia, China—or, as it is officially called, the People's Republic of China—is undoubtedly one of the most powerful nations in the world in all imaginable aspects. In fact, due to its remarkable growth since the end of the last century, most clearly characterized by great economic, military, social, and technological advancements, many political science scholars and experts consider China the new most dominant country in the world—taking this title from the United States, largely believed to have held this position since World War I.

Whether this assertion is true or not, one thing is undeniable—Chinese history is one of the most exciting and compelling, spanning back thousands of years to the beginning of the first human civilizations around its great rivers, Huang He and Yangtze, some of which date as far back as the 10th millennium BCE. For thousands of years, the Chinese have settled the lands in East Asia, developing in parallel to their counterparts in Mesopotamia and the Indus during the ancient era and giving birth to one of the most fascinating and thriving cultures found anywhere in the world. Progressing through ancient times as cultural and technological pioneers, the Chinese continuously evolved and adapted to the changing world dynamic. This eventually led to the nation's formation and its exalted status today. Filled with unique developments and events that continue to spark fascination in every person who endeavors to study it, Chinese history provides a satisfactory experience to curious people of all ages and interests.

This book will cover the most recent part of the long history of China and the Chinese people, focusing on modern times—which, in China, starts with the collapse of the Qing dynasty in the early 20th century. Although this 120-year period may seem short considering the thousands of years of developments that preceded it, the 20th century and the first two decades of the 21st century are packed with just as many vital events that, some would argue, have had the most defining impact on China. Indeed, the 20th century was an era of changes not only in China but also the rest of the world, with many socio-cultural developments drastically transforming the political and social landscapes of many different nations around the globe, not to mention two of the bloodiest wars in a span of roughly 30 years. Understanding the history of modern China is crucial to understanding the country's unique position today and also provides an amazing narrative of China's developing relations with the rest of the world—something that has become increasingly important in the 21st century.

This book will therefore open with a description of the collapse of the Qing dynasty, the events that precipitated it, and the formation of the first republic in China—putting an end to over three thousand years of dynastic rule in Chinese lands. It will look at key occurrences, such as the series of revolutions beginning in 1894 and culminating in the 1911 Xinhai Revolution and the overthrow of the last emperor, Xuantong. As we will see, the processes that caused the downfall of the Qing dynasty and the establishment of a republican regime played a big role in later developments of the century and are considered the beginning of "modern times" in China.

The middle part of the book focuses on the rise of the Communists in China and the country's subsequent transformation from a republic to a Communist-led totalitarian regime. This period begins with the formation of the Chinese Communist Party—the infamous CCP—in 1921, which still holds power in the country 100 years after its inception and more than 70 years after it took power in the revolution of 1949. Of course, the Communist takeover is the biggest event in modern Chinese history and has greatly affected the nation in all regards. We will extensively cover the rule of Mao Zedong—by far one of the most influential figures in Chinese history and often referred to as the founding father of the People's Republic. In his controversial period as the head of the CCP, China made its first efforts towards industrialization, trying to mimic the scale of other prosperous nations around the world. But it also resulted in one of the world's most gruesome and tyrannical regimes, leading to millions dying of starvation and oppression.

Finally, the book will cover the most recent stage of modern Chinese history, roughly starting with the death of Mao Zedong in 1976 and culminating with China's transformation into a global superpower. The increasingly effective policies of the CCP since the end of the 1970s would initiate the Chinese economy's exponential growth by opening to international markets, with the country becoming the fastest-growing market by the beginning of the 21st century. Many social and foreign policy decisions undertaken during this era persist and shape the country's image even today. Concluding with the controversial President Xi Jinping, who took office in 2013, we will look at China's journey from a backwards country unable to use its vast resources to challenge world powers to one of the most advanced—and, at the same time, feared—nations in the world.

Chapter One – The Fall of the Qing Dynasty

Problems of the Dynastic Regime

In 1895, after about a year of conflict, China decisively lost the Sino-Japanese War, signing the Treaty of Shimonoseki in April and ceding the island of Taiwan and parts of contested Southern Manchuria to the Japanese, in addition to paying war reparations. The war was another indication of a fact widely recognized by that time, even by the Chinese people themselves: China was not strong enough to compete with the newly-emerged great powers of the world. The 19th century was an era of modernization throughout Europe, not only of technology (which accounted for most of Europe's superiority) but also of social and economic structures. This eventually led to the development of nationalism as a prominent philosophy and the subsequent creation of nation-states, the most prosperous of which had been increasingly liberal.

As the Europeans were advancing and gaining an advantage over their Asian counterparts, China, with its conservative Qing dynasty, was reluctant to adapt to many of the changes. Ultimately, this reluctance and the imposition of stricter dynastic control had contributed to China's backwardness compared to not only the power-hungry Europeans, who had shown great interest in colonization and meddling with Chinese affairs, but also the rival neighboring country of Japan—a once-conservative Asian nation that had embraced Western ideals and had industrialized to overtake a much larger China in almost all aspects of life.

The devastating defeat and humiliation that followed the land concessions to the Japanese again demonstrated China's need to keep up and make the necessary changes to be at least capable of contesting its enemies in the future. The head of state at the time, at least nominally, was the Guangxu Emperor, who had succeeded as emperor at the age of four in 1875 and had come of age to rule in 1888-1889. During this time, the real power in China was held by the emperor's aunt, Empress Dowager Cixi, a long-standing proponent of the traditional conservative regime and one of the most powerful female figures in all of Chinese history. While Cixi had officially retired from her regency when Guangxu came of age, the Guangxu Emperor was not exactly as competent a ruler as his regent. He was keen on reading and had limited experience in leading, traits that became especially apparent during the war. The ineffective reign of the young emperor and recognition of many of the country's problems eventually motivated many of China's more educated scholars to start thinking about the challenges their country faced in hopes of coming up with solutions that would positively affect its course.

If its defeat in the war was not enough, China also quickly became engulfed in complex diplomatic play with interested European powers, who did not exactly condone the terms of the Treaty of Shimonoseki. The seizure of the Liaotung province in southern Manchuria particularly alarmed the Russians, who wanted the warm waters of the region for themselves to establish a permanent presence in the Pacific. With the help of Germany and France (both nations as interested actors), Russia and the international community forced Japan to reluctantly return control of Liaotung to China. The province's return was seen in China as a silver lining, a product of the efforts of Chinese Grand Secretary Li Hung-chang (Li Hongzhang), who sought to pacify at least some of the discontent in his country after its humiliating defeat at the hands of the Japanese. However, the grand secretary also agreed to the Sino-Russian Secret Treaty in 1896, which allowed the Russians exclusive rights to build railways in the region, use Chinese ports for its navy, and even station troops in Chinese territory.

The increased influence of Russia on China was perceived as a threat to Great Britain and its interests. Britain was the most powerful nation in the world at that time, and it saw China as a barrier to Russian expansion in East Asia. Britain was especially concerned as the European nations arranged themselves in complex alliances with each other to swing the balance of power in their favor, trying to reduce Britain's power. This was further confirmed when, in June of 1897, France managed to strike a deal with China, gaining its own mining rights and treaty port in south China by taking Guangzhouwan. British efforts to kill the deal were countered by firm Russian support, as France and Russia had become allies. Therefore, to ensure its influence in the region would not be completely reduced, Britain allied with Japan in 1902, complicating the power dynamic and contributing to China's suffocation by foreign powers.

Finally, there was also Germany, which became increasingly involved in the situation after the murder of two German Catholic missionaries in November of 1897 by an anti-Christian Chinese mob in Jiaozhou (Kiautschou, Kiaochow) Bay. German Emperor Kaiser Wilhelm had long been eyeing a treaty port in China. So, four months after the murder of the German priests, he negotiated a 99-year lease with the Chinese government, taking control of the bay and its surrounding areas. Eventually, all these concessions had a domino effect, leading to the lease of more and more Chinese treaty ports to European nations, significantly increasing their presence in the region. By the beginning of the 20th century, the Germans, British, French, and Russians had significantly overpowered the Chinese, who were forced to watch as foreigners took their lands without much opposition. The "scramble for concessions," as this period is sometimes called, increased the anti-foreign sentiment that had existed in China for a few centuries—which, in turn, became one of the biggest problems for the Qing dynasty to deal with.

A Drive for Reform and Reaction

A man who quickly became a leading thinker in Chinese modernization was Kang Youwei, an advocate for a more liberal, constitutional monarchy resembling the Meiji regime in Japan, which had greatly contributed to that country's rapid transformation. In the 1880s, he had developed an almost critical, revisionist account of Confucianism—the central philosophy upon which much of the social, legislative, and cultural systems of Qing China had been founded. Extensively studying the Confucian texts, Kang and many similar reformists of the time, advocated for a China that would still be fundamentally based on Confucian values and conduct but also utilize many Western developments, especially regarding technology. Later, he concentrated more on creating an idealistic utopia, which he essentially stated in his book, *Ta t'ung Shu* (sometimes translated as *The Great Unity*). In short, by the time the war against Japan ended, Kang Youwei had become a very important and popular thinker, ultimately resulting in his meeting with the Guangxu Emperor and his court in 1898.

Kang's consultations with the young emperor went swimmingly, resulting in the proclamation of an ambitious reform plan that sought to modernize China by touching many aspects of its social and economic life. Through his reinterpretation of Confucius as a man who advocated reform, Kang convinced the monarch and his court of the cultural necessity of modernization and China's practical need for it compared to other countries. The prominence he had gained through his writings, which were heavily distributed among the intelligentsia of the major Chinese cities, certainly helped make the necessity to reform more urgent.

The edict, issued on June 11, 1898, and the subsequent drive for reform became known in history as the Hundred Days' Reform: it would only last until mid-September of the same year when powerful political figures would oppose and overpower it. For three months, the Guangxu Emperor and his reform-minded team drew up changes that focused on creating a new educational system. The state would finance the construction of schools that would teach agriculture, modern sciences, mathematics, and other subjects taught in Western schools instead of solely focusing on giving the students a Confucian education. The reformers also sought to move on from the older style of examination widely used in China to instead focus on the students' knowledge of current events in addition to history and classical Chinese works. They believed an effective education system was one of the most important institutions in the world and directly translated to the creation of more competent citizens who would be more effective in every job they undertook. In addition to revamping the country's disorganized education system, the decree also envisioned a complete reorganization of the state administration, where corrupt officials held obscure, useless jobs and were paid directly from the treasury. Eliminating these positions, also called sinecures, would make the government much more effective while costing less for upkeep. The reformers also prepared to make changes to the country's agricultural and industrial sectors. These included the state's assumption of unused fertile lands for farming and the creation of bureaus for manufacturing railways and mining.

In the end, however, many conservatives voiced harsh opposition to the initiative before any of the reforms could be properly implemented. Those whose positions were being abolished, such as some military and state officials, and students who had seemingly studied their whole lives for nothing, protested the most. The conservative elite's response was much more cohesive. They believed implementing these westernizing reforms would be denouncing China's culture and its superiority to the deranged Western ideals of the European countries that had been hostile towards the Chinese, seeking to exploit the country's resources for their own good. Many held that the Chinese people did not deserve the complete abandonment of their culture, especially in favor of embracing the enemy.

A significant part of the stern opposition to the Hundred Days Reform was due to the fact that many powerful ministers, state officials, and military commanders were still loyal to Empress Dowager Cixi and had waited to see her reaction to the radical changes the emperor planned to implement. Although she had formally retired to her lavish Summer Palace, Cixi was still arguably the most influential person in the country, especially since the emperor had no real governing experience and had started his reign with an unfortunate defeat against the Japanese. Thus, as more and more people opposed the proposed reforms, Cixi felt compelled to act, not only for the country's best interests but also for herself—as the reforms sought to substantially increase the acting government's power by taking away influence from the royal family. Putting the conservative Manchu general Ronglu in charge of a small force, she staged a coup d'état, denouncing her nephew's actions and effectively stripping Guangxu of his powers as the monarch. She then put him under house arrest in the palace, where the emperor would spend the rest of his days until his death in 1908. After that, Cixi and her supporters cracked down on all the radicals in favor of the reforms, arresting and executing many liberals. Kang Youwei, the main proponent of Chinese liberalization and modernization, managed to escape the empress dowager, fleeing to Japan but never ceasing his political involvement. The Hundred Days' Reform was thus dead. The conservatives had triumphed in China.

The Boxer Movement

The conservative reaction to the reform efforts is perhaps best characterized by the events that followed Empress Dowager Cixi's coup as part of a movement that started in late 1898. Cixi's influence was restored with the coup, and many liberal-minded forces within the country were undermined immediately following the Hundred Days' Reform. The crackdown on pro-Western forces and the increased presence of foreign powers in various Chinese coastal provinces produced a very strong, violent reaction from the masses, who had been greatly struggling during this period. Many had been reduced to extreme poverty due to unfortunate weather conditions and subsequent droughts and floods. People were also growing increasingly hostile towards the Western powers' meddling in local affairs, criticizing their construction of the railways, labor-heavy mining complexes, military presence, and— very importantly—Christian influences, which they believed to be a threat to traditional Confucianism.

Thus, these impoverished and discontent masses, seeking revenge on the Europeans, began forming multiple secret societies, the most prominent of which became the Boxer movement. Operating under the name *I-ho ch'üan* (Yihequan), which translates to "fists of righteousness and harmony" and was a branch of ancient Chinese fighting art, the Boxers aimed to rid their country of foreigners. Eventually, the movement grew so much that it even attracted the attention of several prevalent royal figures, including Empress Dowager Cixi, whose administration later declared its support. After gaining influence, the Boxers were declared a militia force in the province of Shandong, where they had been the strongest. Government officials increasingly used them to protect their interests, trying to suppress anti-traditional forces and undermine foreign presence any way they could.

In the spring of 1900, the Boxer movement would truly gain traction as it engaged relentlessly with Christian communities in different Chinese cities, seeing them as the main proponents of corrupt Western influence on China. The rebellious bands ravaged the countryside, cracking down on what they thought were enemies of the state. Eventually, in June of 1900, as the Boxers reached the capital city of Peking, the foreign powers assembled a joint relief force of 2,100 men to defend their subjects. Acting on the empress dowager's orders, the Boxers and the imperial troops clashed with the foreigners and drove them back before proceeding to Peking. In mid-June, Cixi declared war on all foreign powers in China, stating that the Chinese people had determined the fate of their country and that she was simply trying to uphold the "voices of their hearts." The Boxers in Peking besieged the Peking Legation Quarter, a large part of the city designated exclusively for foreign activities, concentrating their embassies, housing, and churches there. Hundreds of foreign civilians, diplomats, troops, and Chinese Christians were murdered, greatly upsetting the foreign powers, who decided to finally intervene with a concentrated assault.

In August, an international force of about 20,000 strong, including troops from Russia, Great Britain, the US, Japan, Germany, Italy, and France, landed near Peking and started their assault on the city, quickly overpowering the rebels and the imperial guards and taking control of the capital. After about two months of Boxer ravaging and brutal suppression of members of the foreign legation, the siege was finally lifted. Although the number of casualties is disputed, it is estimated that tens of thousands of foreigners, as well as Chinese Christians and Boxers, perished during the rebellion, which was encouraged and promoted by the empress and her court. After taking control of the capital, the foreign powers negotiated with members of the royal family while Cixi fled west. The Boxer Protocol, signed a year later between the two parties, forced China to pay devastating reparations, a total upwards of $330 million over 40 years.

All in all, the Boxer rebellion of 1900 was a very significant point in the late Qing era, setting the stage for the ultimate Revolution of 1911, which caused the collapse of the dynastic regime in China. Rooted in xenophobia, terrible living conditions, and a series of unfortunate events, the Boxer movement had devastating consequences for China's status on the world stage, allowing for continued foreign intervention in the coming decade.

Setting the Stage for Revolution

The Boxer Rebellion had done more harm than good to the Chinese people. With international armies occupying the country's capital and Empress Dowager Cixi having fled Peking, it seemed as if China was about to be "officially" colonized, divided among the foreign powers like Africa had been a few decades earlier. Foreign spheres of influence did not become formal colonies, although there certainly was a pretext for a full-scale invasion, as the richest parts of the country were already under foreign control. Still, due to China's sheer size, heavy opposition from the local population, and the new US "Open Door Policy," which proclaimed the various powers should allow each other to conduct business in their spheres of influence, China's independence was preserved. Cixi remained the empress dowager and, after many more concessions and international pressure, was forced to introduce some liberal reforms.

Empress Dowager Cixi.
https://commons.wikimedia.org/wiki/File:The_Ci-Xi_Imperial_Dowager_Empress_(6).PNG

Thus, in the years following the Boxer Rebellion, China slowly began to transform. New military reforms modernized the army, with the experienced general Yuan Shikai, who had maneuvered his way to power by 1901 when Cixi's reforms first started, leading the process. With a reorganized army of nearly 60,000 trained personnel by 1904, Yuan Shikai had the biggest and the most professional force in the country at his disposal. He essentially controlled the territories surrounding the capital—which gave him tremendous influence and power. The empress dowager's court also negotiated new deals with foreign powers regarding trade customs and tariffs, especially on products that were heavily in demand, like opium. The administrative system was improved, and new remote territories were finally taxed after years of being disconnected from the central government. The newly-appointed provincial governors built new educational institutions and sent their most successful students to study abroad and get a foreign education. Many changes were made to the domestic education system, with modernization in mind according to European principles. These changes were just the first step in China's long-standing goal of catching up with the rest of the world and utilizing its potential.

However, the new changes did come at a cost to the Qing government. In the end, the rapid efforts of modernization caused a greater decentralization of power, and the upper classes, which had disproportionately ruled most of the country, came increasingly under scrutiny. The new education system had allowed Western principles to reach a larger audience; more people became aware of the changes and wanted even greater reforms. Due to a more liberalized press, republican ideas became more prominent among average citizens, often denied representation by the high-class Manchu gentry who still controlled the more powerful channels of government. Soon, anti-Qing sentiment began to rise in the population. This was amplified by the increased power of the regional leaders, who had each assumed more influence due to the overall decentralization of the system, backed by their own armies and supporters.

Alongside Yuan Shikai, who controlled many northern Chinese lands with his own loyal army, there was also a powerful regional leader in Wuhan named Zhang Zhidong. Both leaders were similarly in charge of devoted followers and had assumed considerable power that almost made them on par with the central government—which alarmed the Qing court.

However, the person who would play a key role in forming a Chinese republic was a Methodist from Guangdong named Sun Yat-sen. Born in the southeastern region of the country where he'd been exposed to British Hong Kong from an early age and educated in British and American schools in Hawaii, Sun Yat-sen had long been an adherent to Western principles. Although he had become a doctor, he was very interested in politics; he was aware of China's problems that kept it from modernizing and ambitious to change them. Eventually, Sun Yat-sen would play a crucial role as a leader of the revolution that would end the Qing dynastic rule in 1911.

Yat-sen's career in politics had humble beginnings, however. He decided to fully drop medicine in the early 1890s and move to Honolulu to found an organization named Revive China Society, which would ultimately emerge as one of the most prominent revolutionary movements in the first decade of the 20th century. Sun Yat-sen and his republic-minded supporters had even tried to revolt against the Qing in Guangzhou during the Sino-Japanese War, ending in the forced exile of the young leader from his country. During his time abroad, especially in England, Sun Yat-sen further indulged himself in liberal readings, reinforcing his own ideas of Chinese republicanism. Upon his return to Asia in 1903, he sought to lead a republican wave of supporters to finally set China on its destined path of Westernization.

The Revolution of 1911

As the Qing dynasty was introducing several ambitious reform programs (and, subsequently, fueled an anti-monarchist movement in the country), the first decade of the 20th century saw uprisings in various provinces that wished to undermine local royal influence. The Qing forces quelled the revolts, often arresting and executing the rebels by the thousands, but the rebellions demonstrated that the country had become increasingly liberal and had recognized the hardships it experienced compared to other advanced nations. The Chinese people became aware they were being actively exploited by foreign powers and blamed the royal family. An event that shocked the whole country was the strange death of the Guangxu Emperor in 1908, followed a day later by the death of Empress Dowager Cixi. The mysterious circumstances in which two of the most prominent members of the Qing perished alarmed many forces in the country and resulted in the exile of Yuan Shikai, who had been condemned to execution by the will of the emperor but had avoided his punishment with the help of his allies in court. The general had close ties with the empress dowager, starting from the coup of 1898 when they overthrew the emperor during the Hundred Days' Reform. The two are suspected of having poisoned Guangxu, as in 2008, an expert found abnormal arsenic levels in his remains. Thus, the Qing monarchy was in a complete uproar—fighting provincial rebels on top of having to deal with the death of its leaders—when the final crisis that led to its demise took place.

By early 1911, China had an extensive railway network in its eastern provinces, but the most crucial areas of it were under the control of foreign powers due to decades of concessions from the Qing government. Over time, several provincial rail lines were returned to local governments, especially in the southern and western parts of the country, which had started to develop and profit from them even more, injecting their own capital into the projects. Despite their efforts, it was clear that much of the money raised by the local governments was not being properly spent but lost to corruption while the railways were not built. This eventually led the central government to nationalize the building and control of the country's railways in 1911, with Peking obtaining a foreign loan to finance the endeavor.

The reaction to the government's decision ultimately lit the final spark for revolution and produced a more-or-less united response from forces within the country that had already strived to end the monarchy. Protests broke out in different provinces, most notably in Sichuan, where the local gentry organized their supporters into the "railway protection" movement, trying to undermine the central government. In many instances, local rulers directly ordered people to go on strikes, which turned more and more into violent clashes with royalist forces that were ordered to quell the revolts. Of course, the local gentry, who had directly invested and stolen money in the process of building railways, were upset with the nationalization because it directly threatened their stable source of income and influence. In addition, they propagated the idea that, since the government's actions were financed with foreign loans, foreign powers would inevitably become more powerful in China once again, exploiting the country and its people as they had done for ages. This ignited the xenophobic-traditionalist sentiments that still existed in most of the population. Along with hatred towards the Qing regime and the unfortunate circumstances it had brought, this resulted in a revolutionary movement that managed to overthrow the monarchy by the end of the year.

It is difficult to accurately convey the scale of the protests that erupted throughout the country since all the provinces were engulfed in general unrest. By late September, the number of revolutionaries had grown, with revolutionary sentiments penetrating the ranks of the Qing army stationed in Wuhan. This eventually led to a mutiny within the Wuhan corps in early October 1911. The revolutionaries managed to gain control of the region and its supplies and declare them no longer under the jurisdiction and control of the Qing monarchy in Peking. Although many of the key mutineers had been arrested by royalist forces, those who remained elected Li Yuanhong, a relatively inexperienced colonel, to lead them—a person who would eventually emerge as a president of the newly-born Chinese Republic. Crucially, after the mutiny, the revolutionaries managed to gain the support of Yuan Shikai, who decided to come out of his "retirement" and reinforced the revolutionaries in Wuhan using his great influence and the means he had controlled while at the height of his power.

This movement was weaker and more disorganized than other Chinese revolutionary groups in China and outside its borders. While the revolutionaries' motivation and justification for revolution greatly differed, they got increasingly into contact with each other. By November 1911, when Yuan Shikai was elected as the new prime minister, they were largely united under the same banner. In addition to the mutineers of Wuhan and Yuan Shikai's men, there was also Sun Yat-sen's Revive China Society and the Tongmenghui, a larger secret Chinese nationalist society with origins in Japan, and many smaller groups that, nevertheless, brought thousands of supporters to join the cause.

These different revolutionary groups would finally assemble in late 1911 in Nanking. Discussing the situation in the country, they recognized that the Qing government had no real means of stopping the movement, as the main army corps was no longer under the monarchy's control. The leaders of the revolutionaries thus agreed to set up a provisional government in Nanking and proclaim the first Chinese Republic, electing Sun Yat-sen as the first president on January 1, 1912.

Chapter Two – The Early Chinese Republic

The Beiyiang Era

The Revolution of 1911 in China is immensely significant due to its political consequences and arguably one of the most unique large-scale revolutions to take place during the era of nationalism. This uniqueness is based on the fact that there had been grounds for revolution in China at least decades before its eventual reality. (The Hundred Days' Reform is a good example of an event that could have led to a liberalized constitutional monarchy as a diverging path from the country's old-fashioned, autocratic regime.) However, due to the scale of the country territorially and in terms of population, it was very difficult to organize a united front against the Qing monarchy—as opposed to Europe, where far fewer people needed to be involved in the nationalist drive to force a regime change. In fact, many historians believe that this factor was the biggest detriment for the Chinese people when organizing a revolution. Due to this same "largeness" factor, the revolutionary movement was disjointed and, immediately after its triumph in late 1911, produced a system that was not nearly as effective as it could have been. In short, although Sun Yat-sen and other revolutionary leaders and liberal thinkers had created a framework of Chinese liberal nationalism against the Qing dynasty, logistically speaking, they encountered far more problems in making their ideas come to fruition.

During their first assemblies in Nanking, the revolutionaries deemed themselves the provisionary government and tried to figure out how exactly to gain power from the monarchy in a legitimate way. Another issue was that different provinces had declared independence from the Qing monarchy during the revolutionary uprisings, and the new government would ultimately need to reassert its control over them. In fact, 15 out of the 24 Qing provinces had declared their independence from the central government, giving the revolutionaries a significant advantage.

The first problem was easily dealt with, at least on paper. Yuan Shikai, commanding the largest and strongest force in the country, known as the Beiyang Army, arrived in Peking in February, forcing the final Qing emperor, Puyi, to abdicate in favor of a republic. This happened while the bulk of the revolutionaries, including the newly-elected provisional president Sun Yat-sen, were still in Nanking. The provisional government had also drawn up the first constitution, creating a bicameral legislative body consisting of a parliament and a senate, whose members would be elected for three-year terms through a complex electoral college voting system. Ministries were also set up to govern different aspects of Chinese life under the new regime. In short, the provisional government tried to do what every provisional government does—introduce several institutions to keep the country running. However, it soon became clear that these institutions would be effectively rendered useless in a heavily decentralized and underdeveloped country and that personal and factional power would take over in a regime that was supposed to be democratic.

After the revolutionaries forced the emperor to abdicate, Yuan Shikai became the new provisional president of the republic in Peking in March of 1912. Sun Yat-sen had resigned from his position to actively pursue political life as a member of his party—the Chinese Nationalist Party, or the Kuomintang (KMT).[1]

---

[1] Also sometimes spelled as *Guomindang (GMD)*

Yuan Shikai as President of the republic, 1915. Photo by Rio V. De Sieux.
https://commons.wikimedia.org/wiki/File:YuanShikaiPresidente1915.jpg

The reason behind this transfer of power can only be explained in terms of actual power held by the individuals. Yuan Shikai was an experienced and well-known commander of the strongest army in the country, while Sun Yat-sen was a doctor-turned-visionary whose job, largely speaking, was complete: the revolutionary movement had triumphed. Sun Yat-sen did not even lead his own party anymore, with Song Jiaoren instead emerging as the new party leader. After Sun Yat-sen stepped down, everyone soon realized that the president held the real power, not least because he personally controlled the revolutionary forces (although the KMT would get the most votes in the first parliament elections). A bigger problem was the fact that only a small portion of the Chinese population was eligible to vote in the elections of 1912-1913, meaning that elected parliament officials had limited authority and legitimacy in the country.

The years following Yuan Shikai's election as the new president came to be known as the Beiyang era, and it is not hard to see why. The president assumed almost complete (although rather ineffective, in hindsight) control of the state, disregarding the political institutions and dragging the country into a period of crisis much like the latter years of Qing rule. After quarreling with the president, KMT leader Song Jiaoren was assassinated under mysterious circumstances, with many blaming Shikai. Using the army at his disposal, Yuan Shikai then intimidated his way to being reelected as president for a set five-year term in October. This came after suppressing a reactionary KMT revolt, also known as the Second Revolution, during which some of the country's southern provinces, led by Sun Yat-sen, had revolted against the president's tyrannical conduct. Many leaders of the movement were arrested and executed by Yuan Shikai, while Sun Yat-sen managed to flee to Japan in November of the same year.

By the time he had dealt with the rebellion, Yuan Shikai had cemented himself as essentially a new autocratic ruler of China, acting completely independently and always disregarding the parliament when making political decisions. For example, he notably borrowed an egregious sum of 25 million pounds from foreign banks without consulting the parliament, which he would ultimately dissolve after being reelected as president in early 1914. A month later, in true autocratic fashion, Yuan Shikai called a new assembly to revise the constitution, granting him an array of new privileges that amounted to virtually unlimited power. As if these decisions were not enough, in late 1915, Yuan Shikai overreached. Confident that he held a strong grip over the country and was supported by his court, he declared himself the new emperor of China, ending the short-lived republic established in 1911.

However, unfortunately for the emperor, this move proved fatal to his tenure in power. By the time he became emperor, public sentiment had shifted overwhelmingly against him. So, although he technically gave himself no new privileges after becoming emperor, Yuan Shikai's announcement revived the anti-monarchy feelings that were still prominent among the Chinese. In addition, Shikai's control over most of the country had never truly been that firm: yes, he exercised complete control over the state's political and economic affairs, but his rule only roughly extended to those provinces close to the capital, and he rarely left Peking. In more rural areas of the country, the central government's authority was almost nonexistent, and the provincial gentry were still the most influential actors, posing a great threat to Yuan Shikai's aspirations.

Finally, Shikai's self-proclamation as emperor was the last straw for many of his generals, who had largely remained loyal to him during his lavish endeavors but finally had enough of Yuan's selfish decisions. After all, most members of his army had fought to overthrow the corrupt and autocratic Qing rule, so seeing their commander become so much like their enemy was a horrifying sight.

All this sentiment against Yuan Shikai manifested in an increased number of public revolts and uprisings, the most important of which was the National Protection War, waged by several prominent provincial leaders against the self-declared emperor. Originating in the southern province of Yunnan and spreading to include most southern and central territories of the country, the National Protection Movement, with the help of Yuan Shikai's generals, managed to triumph over the emperor, forcing him to abdicate in March of 1916. This was essentially the second revolution in five years. Yuan Shikai would die in June of the same year, having played an infamous role in modern Chinese history. His position would be assumed by vice-president Li Yuanhong, and the republican regime would finally be restored.

The Warlord Era

The years following Yuan Shikai's abdication and the republic's restoration were very chaotic. The collapse of Yuan's regime shed light on some fundamental problems that had existed for a long time but had been ignored for various reasons. The most prominent of these problems was that the central government's authority barely spread to the more remote provinces of China, creating a power vacuum that greatly halted the development of the country and the realization of its goals and aspirations. Since the mid-1910s, after the overthrow of Yuan, the country was thus essentially divided by different powerful actors that undermined the power held by President Li Yuanhong. He was the country's leader only nominally; in reality, different regions were basically ruled by generals who exercised their authority over the people. These years would come to be known as the Warlord Era.

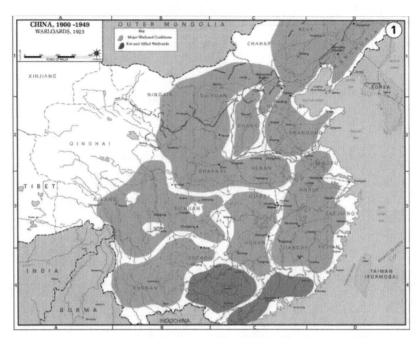

Warlord Era divisions in China, 1925. U.S. Army.

https://commons.wikimedia.org/wiki/File:Map_of_major_Chinese_warlord_coalitions_1925.png

Indeed, the duties of the central government, president and prime minister included, were limited to having formal relations with foreign countries, while the real power inside China was up for grabs. However, the new government's tenure coincided with one of the most influential events of the 20th century—World War I—allowing it to take measures that may have been impossible at any other time. Indeed, the Chinese central government even contemplated joining the war on the Allies' side due to the more significant French, Japanese, Russian, and British presence in its territories than that of Germany. The main advocate for Chinese entry into the war was Prime Minister Duan Qirui, leader of the regional Anhui clique faction, who eventually persuaded the parliament to cut its ties with the Germans. He was eventually exposed for a scandal that involved loans given to him by the Japanese to act according to their interests in China. Although President Li Yuanhong tried to remove him from office because of this, many generals under Duan's influence opposed this move, keeping Duan Qirui as prime minister.

An interesting development in the years immediately after the restoration of the republic was a brief royalist effort to restore Emperor Puyi to the throne as a Qing monarch. In fact, in July of 1917, utilizing the chaos created by Duan Qirui's opposition in Peking, royalist General Zhang Xun managed to take control of the capital, forcing President Li Yuanhong to flee to the protection of the French and Japanese legations. The royalists declared Puyi the new emperor of China and canceled the republic, dissolving the parliament, but their "victory" did not last long. In less than two weeks, taking control of the republican forces in Tianjin, the prime minister ordered an assault on the Forbidden City and assumed power again. On July 12, the Manchu Restoration, as the event came to be known, ended.

A series of further chaotic developments ensued after the failed attempt of the royalists to bring back the monarchy. Duan Qirui, still holding the most power in the country, refused to restore the old parliament in favor of forming a new legislative body and soon emerged as a de-facto leader of China. Essentially, he had become the new dictator. Even as Feng Guozhang succeeded Li Yuanhong as president, Qirui could not be denied the power he held. He ruled over a fragmented country, controlling the military and having the most money of all the regional powers. This gave him a sense of clear superiority over anyone who dared challenge his regime.

Meanwhile, the central government had been rendered useless, as the parliament effectively served no function. The elections in 1918 were rigged in favor of Duan Qirui's supporters, who assumed an overwhelming majority and did not interfere with the prime minister's actions. The country was divided among different actors who all strived to gain more influence and power, resulting in tens or hundreds of thousands of killings. The common people, enraged by the dismal conditions they had to endure, often rose up against the Manchu elite. Using the army to remain in power, the latter suppressed the rebels, even those they suspected of being involved in anti-elitist conspiracies.

These problems were also clearly reflected geopolitically, as China temporarily lost control of the provinces of Tibet and Xinjiang and was forced to permanently let go of Outer Mongolia. All these ethnically-different regions, with their own cultures and identities, had long been part of the Chinese empire and comprised a significant portion of its territory, population, and resources. These provinces used the unstable situation in China to declare independence and break away, leading to complex and obscure political landscapes. International actors such as Great Britain had to get involved to avoid further conflict and bloodshed. Mongolia was eventually invaded by the newly-formed Soviet government in 1920 and became the Mongolian People's Republic in 1924. The warlord era was, in short, a disaster for the Chinese nation and its people in almost every aspect. Only a handful of individuals managed to benefit from the system, expanding their power and exploiting the chaotic situation that had arisen in the country.

The May Fourth Movement

Parallel to the political chaos that had ensued in China ever since the 1911 revolution, there also seems to have been a cultural movement that managed to gain traction in the early years of the republic. The "New Culture Movement" built on the revisionist accounts of traditional Confucianism and the late Qing efforts aimed at modernization and sought to transform Chinese political and social life into one that adhered to Western principles of freedom and democracy. In their mission to promote democracy and Western values, however, the supporters of the New Culture Movement were relatively limited. The decentralized power structure did not allow for a cohesive agenda and course of action for the reform-minded, and getting these ideas to most of the Chinese population still posed a significant problem. Most people were under-educated peasants who did not live in urban areas throughout the country. They had no time to worry about adopting Western ideas, let alone trying to thoroughly understand them. Meanwhile, the authoritarian elite, led by the premier and leader of the Anhui clique Duan Qirui, vehemently opposed anything that could have undermined their power and status.

For these reasons, the New Culture Movement was subtle; it needed a triggering event to elevate its relevance and push it into the mainstream political climate. That triggering event would eventually come in May of 1919 and would have immense social and political implications for years to come. By early 1919, the instability and unrest in the country had reached their peak due to several prior developments. First, word spread of the secret Sino-Japanese Joint Defense Agreement, giving Japan large concessions, including the privilege to have troops stationed in northern Chinese territories. Unbeknownst to the public and many people in power, the pro-Japanese Duan Qirui had negotiated the deal in exchange for bribes and loans from Japan.

There were also the Chinese diplomatic failures during the negotiations after World War I. These were dominated by the interests of the victorious Great Powers, who largely overlooked Chinese demands during the meetings in Versailles even though China had contributed to the war effort on the Allies' side. The Chinese delegation had demanded the return of Shandong (a German-held territory in China whose control was transferred to Japan after the war) and the termination of any type of foreign power involvement in China, including treaty ports held by countries like Britain and France. In the end, despite technically being one of the victors of the war, China got nothing from the Treaty of Versailles. The delegation came home empty-handed, disappointing a local population that had seen its country effectively send tens of thousands of soldiers to war for nothing. These developments fueled the already-existing distrustful sentiment towards the central government by clearly pointing out its inability to act effectively for national interests on the international stage and produced the immensely influential "May Fourth Movement."

In early May 1919, the students would lead the troubled populace and try to voice their concerns by organizing mass protests—first in Peking and then all throughout the country. The movement soon gained traction, as the nationalist, anti-government, and progressive principles advocated by the protesters attracted many supporters. The central government's response was mass arrests throughout the movement's duration, but this did not dissuade the protesters from emerging even stronger. As more people of different classes and mindsets joined the protests in the mid-to-late stages of the protests, the movement's focus shifted from students to middle and low-class workers, who had used the opportunity to go on strikes against their poor working conditions. This shift became especially clear when Shanghai became the city with the biggest and the most organized strikes, as the working class was the strongest and the largest there. Realizing the true scale of the protests in such a populous country as China is difficult, and the numbers that describe the movement's members vary significantly. However, the coordinated efforts of the working class, which was a very important part of the Chinese economy and society, completely paralyzed the country and underlined the severity and influence of the movement.

Ultimately, the May Fourth Movement would have political, social, and cultural implications that would affect the Chinese nation for decades. First, it demonstrated that, due to the sheer number of protesters and the attractiveness of Western principles, the will of the people could overpower the ruling elite that had been perceived as untouchable in the past. In fact, the continued protests pressured the central government to release many of the activists who had been arrested initially. It also showed that only the common people, not the numerically inferior members of the higher classes who had regarded themselves as inherently superior, could usher economic and social modernization into China. Chinese society had to become more egalitarian—there was no debate about that. Many had taken up European principles of freedom and democracy simply because they gave commoners a voice—people who had been struggling for decades, working in exploitative conditions, living in terrible houses in rural and urban areas, and existing in extreme poverty that was simply unacceptable. The May Fourth Movement also put a greater emphasis on the modernization and general importance of education and produced a cultural response that made it easier for the under-educated population to learn how to read and write. Many authors started to write in the language spoken more commonly and thus more attractive to those who could hardly understand the "higher" forms of Chinese. Focusing on social issues, the authors further demonstrated the country's ills to many who were oblivious to what was happening. Perhaps most importantly, however, the May Fourth Movement is often regarded as a precursor to the Communist movement: the ideas and goals of the protests would, in the following years, be modified to promote Marxist principles in Chinese society.

Chapter Three – The Chinese Communist Party

The Birth of Chinese Communism

The May Fourth Movement, as discussed above, had a significant social impact on the Chinese people, promoting social and political liberalization and pushing for the modernization that would put China on par with its rival nations. It was, in essence, a realization of what many adherents of Western ideology had hoped for decades; eventually, it was seen as a precedent to the rise of Communism in China—an ideology that ultimately came to dominate China's political landscape after the end of World War II and is still present today. However, although vastly influential and consequential, the emergence of Communism in Chinese society was rather slow and gradual. It took a few decades before it became as mainstream as it is today.

With the relative political liberalization that followed the New Culture Movement, especially as it coincided with the decentralized and chaotic time of the warlord era, new political movements slowly emerged and gained traction. One was the Chinese Communist Party (CCP), officially founded in July 1921 in Shanghai. The party's founding was heavily influenced and aided by the recent triumph of the Bolsheviks, who had assumed power in Russia with the revolution of 1917 and, by 1921, had become the most powerful advocates of Communist ideology in the world.

Now, discussing the differences among Communism, socialism, and Russian Leninism requires an in-depth explanation and is certainly beyond the scope of this book. However, it is worth mentioning some of the qualities that differentiate these ideologies and are identified with both the Bolsheviks in Russia and the CCP in China. Generally speaking, Karl Marx is considered the father of Communism, which, in his eyes, was a logical, historically-provided development from socialism—a theory that advocates for the ownership of the means of production and property by society as a whole rather than private individuals. It is often up to interpretation what exactly "society" can stand for in a socialist system, ranging from the state to a simple community. In any case, the Communist (or Marxist) ideology instead asserts that it is an advancement of the socialist system in which the means of production is publicly owned and there is no private property, class, or profit-oriented economy. The needs of every member of society are equally provided to them.

The Communist ideology the Bolsheviks advocated for was a certain interpretation of the Communist ideology proposed by Marx. The leader of the Bolsheviks at the time, Vladimir Lenin, built on the ideas of Marxism but claimed that the only logical transition to a Communist system was by means of a revolution led by the working classes, or the proletariat—the exploited group in a traditional capitalistic society. The Bolsheviks heavily promoted this idea (since deemed Leninism) and gradually seized power in Russia by the turn of the 1920s. Leninist ideology had become the most prominent and successful version of Communism in the world by that time. Thus, going forward, the terms will be used interchangeably.

The Bolsheviks came to power in Russia by claiming they were taking control of the economy from the rich and corrupt Russian elite so that it would, instead, benefit the working class. They gradually regarded the Communist revolution as something that should happen throughout the world. In 1919, the Bolsheviks founded the Communist International (Comintern, sometimes referred to as the Third International), an organization devoted to the spread and promotion of Communism and the coming together of all Communist countries worldwide. Through the Comintern, the Bolsheviks tried to help existing and newly-created socialist movements in different countries, including China, where they were highly influential during the formation of the CCP in 1921.

The Communist movement appealed to many who thought the central government in Peking, with its corrupt elites who had no regard for the good of the people, was exploiting the population for its own interests. Since this sentiment had been rather popular in China for a long time, Communist ideas soon spread throughout the intellectual sphere of China. This became the main proponent of the ideology with assistance from the Russian Bolsheviks and the Comintern.

It is interesting to see and describe the development of Communism in China, as the ideology was new to the country's culture and tradition—Chinese society was as hierarchical as it gets. Historians have recognized that the ideology's traction is a consequence of the unstable, critical situation the country found itself in during the early 1920s. Still, in July 1921, when the CCP first assembled at its first congress, organized by the two main advocates for the spread of Communism in China—Chen Duxiu and Li Dazhao—only 50 members who attended the meeting. Even for the first few years, no more than a thousand people were familiar with Communism and supported it. Most of these were not members of the lowest working classes in the country since they had no real access to institutions where they could get information about it. Eventually, the intellectuals most familiar with the concept of Communism—who recognized that the Chinese workers in the country's early path towards a modern industrial system had poor working conditions, low wages, and other problems that had led to a revolution in Russia and reform in other places—organized the working classes into a proletariat that would strive for changes in the country.

The United Front

One of the first actions of the Chinese Communist Party, with help from the Comintern, was to organize a workers' strike in 1922, which originated in Hong Kong and quickly spread throughout the southern part of the country. The Seamen's Strike was a movement of more than 30,000 workers in Hong Kong who demanded (and eventually received) wage increases from their employers in March of 1922. By organizing themselves into a union, the seamen achieved great success. This was attempted in the coming months among other workers, but with relative failure, as the warlords suppressed the movements efficiently. Still, the seamen's strike was one of the first instances of a Communist-inspired union achieving a small victory over Chinese employers, giving much hope to the adherents of Communism in China.

Crucially, starting in 1922, the CCP and the Comintern engaged in negotiations with Sun Yat-sen's KMT party, which was still operating its own government in Guangzhou, to gain more prominence in the Chinese political scene. These negotiations eventually produced an alliance between the Communists and the KMT, which gave the CCP a lot of exposure; many members of the CCP joined the KMT and vice versa. Ultimately, the two parties emerged as a "United Front" with the intention of coming into power, although their exact motivations were rather vague. For example, the KMT, acting with Sun Yat-sen's agenda, mainly held that Chinese modernization should have been achieved through nationalism, democracy, and the welfare of the people. The KMT did not delve into matters of class struggle as the Communists did, mainly because most of its members came from higher, more privileged classes. Organizing a movement radically against their own class seemed illogical, to say the least. However, after the CCP became affiliated with the KMT, the "welfare" principle of the party's agenda was modified to include aspects of socialism. Through this, the United Front emerged as a prominent alliance between the two parties that mainly sought to create a united democratic national government by ending the warlord-era regional divisions and promoting economic development to help modernize and industrialize the country.

Portrait of Sun Yat-sen. (K.T. Thompson).
https://commons.wikimedia.org/wiki/File:Sun_Yat_Sen_portrait_2_(9to12).jpg

As historians have pointed out, the last aspect of capitalistic economic development went against the principles of the CCP. The whole idea of the Communist revolution adhered to by the Comintern, the Bolsheviks, and the Chinese Communists was to replace the capitalist system, which they believed to be exploitative. Although Lenin and the Bolsheviks had proven that the Communists could take over when a capitalist, industrial system was not present (as was the case in Russia in 1917, which is why the Bolsheviks embarked on an industrialization spree upon their assumption of power), the CCP was far less powerful and influential. The complex political landscape of China, the sheer size of its population, and its involvement in foreign affairs simply did not allow for a Communist revolution on the scale of the Bolsheviks' at that time. Yes, it was true that Lenin and his supporters had also been few, but the Russian Revolution was very different from 1920s China, which was not even a united country and was dominated by far more powerful actors. Thus, the alliance between the KMT and the CCP was not forged because it was truly what the CCP wanted—or, for that matter, what Sun Yat-sen and the KMT desired. Instead, it was a far more practical agreement between the two parties and the Comintern, which was very much interested in the future of Communism throughout the world, especially in such a large country as China. Namely, the CCP gained national recognition as it became affiliated with the famous Sun Yat-sen and the KMT. The KMT managed to grow substantially and gained funding, support, and advice from the Comintern, whose members were far more experienced in assuming power in a country. And the Comintern (or Bolsheviks, if you will), hoped to get the country under a Communist government in exchange for providing assistance to the Chinese, which would be a significant development in the spread of Communism throughout the world—their original goal and intent.

With the help of the Comintern, the KMT and the CCP centered their activities from 1924 onwards in and around the city of Guangzhou in the south. Of course, they did not operate with the central Beiyang government in Peking. Given this opportunity, the KMT was finally able to realize many of its goals since it had previously lacked funding and means to emerge as a more competitive organization. Sun Yat-sen and his allies had long requested financial and arms support from the West, but the Europeans never considered their requests. On the other hand, the Comintern provided substantial aid since the strengthening of the Communist revolutionary movement was in its direct interest. Namely, the Comintern helped create and equip the National Revolutionary Army and a military academy in Whampoa (Huangpu), where most instructors were from Russia. Many members of the KMT and the CCP underwent training in Whampoa, emerging as effective military leaders and learning the principles of revolution and governance from their advisors. The Russians realized that a Communist revolution was not quite possible in China in these circumstances and therefore did not advocate for it as heavily as members of the CCP—a reason behind the Comintern's cordial relations with the KMT. Sun Yat-sen even asserted that Russia was the most trustful friend the United Front possessed, calling it a "teacher in revolution."

The United Front (also known as the KMT-CCP Alliance) would see the first divisions among its ranks after the death of Sun Yat-sen in March of 1925. Since the movement's establishment, the

CCP had been the radical wing of the United Front, while KMT members were more moderate right-wingers who did not exactly buy the idea of a Communist revolution due to the Comintern's advice. These differences manifested when Wang Jingwei assumed leadership—a more left-leaning member of the KMT who favored the CCP more than his predecessor or most members of his party. This, paired with the increased role the CCP would play in the nationwide demonstrations that followed two months later, alarmed many of the moderates. Due to this, the commandant of the Whampoa Military Academy and the leader of the United Front's armed forces, Chiang Kai-shek, decided to take matters into his own hands and crack down on the movement's radical leftist members. In March 1926, as he had already gained enough influence in the academy, he ordered the arrest of many CCP and Comintern officials in an event that became known as the Zhongshan Incident. To justify his actions, Chiang Kai-shek claimed that after the election of Wang Jingwei, the CCP had been planning a conspiracy against him and the rest of the KMT. With the army under his leadership, he managed to suppress those he accused of conspiring before later releasing them, restricting their activities, and assuming control of the movement by forcing Jingwei to go abroad.

Still, this was not enough to reduce the influence of the CCP, which had emerged as a hope to the underprivileged members of the lower classes. The Communists continued to organize workers into unions and motivate them to participate in strikes. Their efforts were especially effective since many of the workers' employers were foreigners, amplifying the already strong anti-foreign sentiments throughout the country. It was, essentially, what the Communists had wanted from the very beginning—the arousal of public will in their favor. The Guangzhou-Hong Kong strikes saw hundreds of thousands of people go to the streets to protest their working conditions. Crucially, they combined their Communist and anti-foreign sentiments with a nationalist drive, giving their demonstrations far more power and impact.

Meanwhile, after assuming unofficial leadership in the party, Chiang Kai-shek and his supporters increasingly pushed for the expansion of the KMT's influence in the north against the warlords.

By the end of 1925, the United Front had only spread in the southern provinces of Guangdong (where it had originated in the city of Guangzhou) and Guangxi, whereas most Chinese political power was concentrated further to the north. Although many people were skeptical of the military power at the disposal of Chiang Kai-shek, believing it was no match for the warlord forces of the north, the KMT leader believed otherwise. The support the Comintern had given to the party, he and his supporters thought, was enough to overpower the numerically superior armies of the warlords.

The Northern Expedition

Thus, after much preparation and discussion, Chiang Kai-shek, leading an alliance of KMT nationalists and CCP Communists, started his Northern Expedition from Guangzhou in July of 1926, traveling through the eastern provinces with the aim of Chinese unification and the overthrow of the central government. The army, or National Revolutionary Army (NRA), was mainly comprised of KMT nationalists (while the Communists took over the political activities of the movement) and about 250,000 strong by the end of 1926.

Three main groups posed resistance to the United Front—three warlords who each controlled different parts of the country and had many more men than the NRA at the beginning of the campaign. The first, obviously, was the Beiyang government in the north, led by Zhang Zuolin, a warlord from Manchuria and effectively the acting dictator of the central government. Second was a prominent warlord named Sun Chuanfang, leader of the "League of the Five Provinces," which included the eastern and southeastern regions of Fujian, Zhejiang, Anhui, Jiangxi, and Jiangsu. Sun Chuanfang thus essentially controlled the whole eastern part of the country and presented a barrier to the NRA on its expedition. Finally, the third most powerful force the KMT-CCP coalition would have to encounter was led by Wu Peifu, who controlled the three central provinces of Hubei, Hunan, and Henan. All in all, the NRA faced quite a challenge from the very beginning, a challenge that would take a lot of effort to overcome.

Chiang Kai-shek.

Surprisingly, however, the NRA appeared to be much more powerful and effective than many believed. There were three main offensives, all of which found success against the resistance of the warlord armies. The NRA pushed through Hunan, Jiangxi, and Fujian; by August, it had already taken over land south of the Yangzi River. The revolutionaries would encounter the most resistance in Jiangxi, stalling their advance at the city of Nanchang by November 1926. Eventually, the NRA broke through, focusing all its strength east and advancing in Zheijang by February 1927.

It soon became clear that everyone had underestimated the strength and dedication of the revolutionaries, who grew stronger as they took over more and more territories and seized equipment and arms from the opposing forces. Chiang Kai-shek proved his military prowess on the battlefield, constantly outsmarting his opponents and using guerilla tactics and a quicker style of warfare to outmaneuver the heavier, less mobile warlord armies that relied on logistics and supply lines. It must also be said that the warlords were quite disorganized, having regional conflicts among themselves that helped the United Front achieve swift victories in most places. Also, crucially, the captured warlord army contingents the NRA would defeat lacked morale and motivation, whereas the revolutionaries were fighting for a real reason, relatively speaking. This is why thousands of the previous warlord troops would change sides after their capture, which meant the NRA was only growing after months of war.

The Split

However, the revolutionaries showed cracks in their unity in the spring of 1927 once they reached the city of Shanghai. Shanghai was one of the most prosperous cities in China due to its commercial ports and the sheer trade power it had acquired, and taking it would also consolidate the power of the NRA south of the Yangzi River. Taking Shanghai was thus very important. So, when the local Communist unionists inside the city seized power in March before the NRA could reach Shanghai and take it in favor of the revolutionaries, it seemed as if a difficult task for Chiang Kai-shek had already been dealt with. As it turned out, the situation was much more complex. Upon arriving in the city, Chiang Kai-shek saw the local Communist takeover as a sort of power play orchestrated by the CCP to control the city and increase its influence over him. Thus, the KMT general ordered his troops to slaughter thousands of Communists and labor unionists in early April in an event known as the Shanghai Massacre. This atrocity, done to undermine Communist influence in the revolutionary movement, was one of the reasons for the eventual split between the KMT and the CCP, which marked the end of the United Front.

Although Chiang Kai-shek's decision to crack down on Shanghai's Communists acted as a trigger for the separation, it was not the only reason behind the movement's dissolution. Throughout the Northern Expedition, as the revolutionaries took over more territory and became more powerful, there had already been questions about the power dynamics in the United Front, especially regarding the governance of the conquered territories. In fact, it had been clear from the beginning that many members of the KMT—especially the far-right-leaning supporters of Chiang Kai-shek—did not share much sympathy for Communist ideas. In their eyes, the CCP-KMT Alliance was simply a means to an end, not the least because many of them were members of the higher classes and supporting Communism would literally mean going against their own. This naturally posed less of a problem when the movement was still young but became much more problematic when the revolutionaries expanded their reach over the southern part of the country. Who and how exactly should govern the people of the conquered provinces? Communist strikes for higher wages in many NRA-controlled cities were increasingly becoming a pressing issue for the leaders of the KMT to deal with. The pro-Chiang wing of the KMT had largely diverted control of political affairs and mobilization of supporters to the CCP before the beginning of the Northern Expedition, and Chiang Kai-shek was more concerned with matters connected to the army and reaching their overall goal. However, as it had been demonstrated, Communism had a lot of appeal among the people—much more support than the KMT general had expected.

Still, the situation was even more complicated than this. Tensions had also existed within the KMT, between Chiang Kai-shek's right-wing nationalist faction and the left-wing non-Communist KMT members led by Wang Jingwei. It would be primarily these members of the party who would establish the new headquarters in the city of Wuhan upon its capture by the NRA in late 1926. Doing so was crucial for centralizing the whole movement, previously based in the remote southern city of Guangzhou, far from the center of the action, which had moved inland with the Northern Expedition. Initially, Chiang Kai-shek and his supporters were also supposed to relocate to Wuhan since they were part of the KMT, but the general instead chose to stay in the city of Nanjing, near Shanghai, where he set up his headquarters in early 1927.

Meanwhile, Wang Jingwei and the left-wing KMT members assembled in Wuhan and held the Third Plenary Session, where they criticized Chiang Kai-shek's leadership of the NRA and his increased hostility towards those he suspected of treason or conspiracy, especially the Communists. Thus, from the beginning of the year 1927, there were essentially three groups in the revolutionary movement: the Communists of the CCP, the left-wing KMT members in Wuhan led by Wang Jingwei (on relatively friendly terms with the CCP), and the more right-leaning nationalist wing of the KMT under Chiang Kai-shek, who also controlled the NRA forces headquartered in Nanjing. Before the Shanghai Massacre, the Wuhan government of Wang Jingwei's leftist KMT members and the CCP denounced Chiang Kai-shek's actions and tried to undermine his power. The leftists in Wuhan believed that the revolutionary cause was starting to better reflect and build upon their ideas and principles rather than those advocated by Chiang Kai-shek.

As mentioned earlier, the tension between the three parties culminated in April 1927 when Chiang Kai-shek slaughtered thousands of Communists, unionists, and left-wing sympathizers in Shanghai, essentially breaking with the rest of the revolutionaries forever. Just six days after the massacre, on April 18, 1927, Chiang Kai-shek officially declared the establishment of a new national government in Nanjing, excluding the CCP and the leftist flank of the KMT. On the same day, Wang Jingwei also gave a public speech in which he heavily criticized Chiang Kai-shek and officially proclaimed the real national government in Wuhan. Thus, the United Front came to an end, with the CCP and the leftist KMT members splitting away from Chiang Kai-shek's right-wing nationalist KMT movement.

Still, this was not the end of the affair. Soon after the dissolution of the United Front, it became clear that the self-declared Wuhan Nationalist Government was also showing cracks between Wang Jingwei's KMT and the CCP. The main reason behind this was the CCP's dependence and the revolutionary movement's overall reliance on support from the Soviet Union and the Comintern. In short, the Russian Soviets, now under the leadership of Joseph Stalin, who was still consolidating his position, had financed the efforts of the CCP since the very beginning. After the coalition with the KMT, they continued to support the movement with the funding and arms crucial to the success of the United Front. The movement was very dependent on Russian support, and Moscow realized this. As soon as the CCP and the left wing of the KMT split from Chiang Kai-shek, however, the Comintern changed its approach to the movement, essentially trying to utilize the disagreement to undermine the authority of Wang Jingwei and the rest of the KMT in Wuhan in favor of the CCP. This became clear less than a month after the split when Stalin issued the "May Instructions," a secret telegram containing messages to guide the party's actions moving forward, to Mikhail Borodin and Manabendra Nath Roy—two Comintern representatives who monitored the actions of the CCP for Moscow. The instructions asserted the following: first, it called for the mass mobilization of Communist workers on strike and peasant sympathizers to raise an army independent of the NRA or whatever Wang Jingwei's KMT could field. Then, it instructed Comintern officials and members of the CCP to try to promote KMT party membership to Communist sympathizers from lower classes to swing the pendulum in CCP's favor during coalition negotiations. Finally, it requested that the CCP gain enough influence in the country to seize entire provinces and get a firm grasp over their people and resources.

Essentially, the May Instructions were the steps outlined by the Comintern for a complete CCP takeover of the still-friendly left wing of the KMT in Wuhan. Stalin had correctly recognized that public sentiment was largely in favor of the Communist cause, made clear by hundreds of worker demonstrations and peasant uprisings around the country. In the eyes of Moscow, the CCP's ultimate victory was only a matter of time—the people just needed to be rallied and put on the same page. While this assertion was partially true, Moscow underestimated the political power and readiness of Wang Jingwei, who quickly became aware of the telegram and saw it as a direct threat to the unity of the Wuhan government. In early June, as word spread of a possible CCP split from the KMT in China, the Comintern requested that the instructions be carried out amid the increased strikes of pro-Communist sympathizers around the country. However, Chen Duxiu, the general secretary of the CCP, pointed out to Moscow that their demands were unrealistic, as the CCP did not quite have the means to do what had been requested by the Comintern. Still, it was too late.

On July 15, after more than a month of political maneuvering between the CCP, the Comintern, Soviet officials in Wuhan, and Wang Jingwei and his supporters, Jingwei finally publicly criticized the May Instructions during a KMT party congress held in Wuhan. He believed that the Comintern had jeopardized the efforts of the revolutionaries by motivating the CCP to split away from the cause and undermine the power of the KMT movement, which had been central to the revolution. Thus, he formally suspended the activities of the Communists in the Wuhan government and expelled the CCP from the coalition. This caused a reactionary response from the Communists, who launched an armed uprising in the city of Nanchang in Jiangxi on August 1, 1927. Military leaders charged with the defense of the city took up arms for the Communist cause, managing to briefly capture the city for the CCP before being forced to retreat as a KMT army was approaching. The Nanchang Uprising is often regarded as the first event in a conflict between the CCP and the KMT that would only fully conclude two decades later in the Chinese Civil War.

Chapter Four – The Nanjing Decade

The Capture of Beijing

The Nanchang Uprising, the final occurrence during the three-way split between the two branches of the KMT and the CCP, had immense political consequences for all three groups. The CCP suffered a heavy blow with the defeat, which many believed was the end of the party and its importance in national affairs. The fiasco at Nanchang was then followed by several other attempted revolts against the KMT armies in big cities like Guangzhou and Changsha, but these were also quelled by the nationalists. The Communist leaders, realizing they did not have the means to fight for big population centers and undermine the emerging KMT dominance, instead retreated to the countryside, essentially going underground but never quite stopping their activities. Widespread support still existed for the appealing Communist cause among the lower classes of China, especially the peasants. This was first recognized by one of the high-ranking CCP members, Mao Zedong, as early as 1926, when the United Front movement was still young. The peasants were by far the largest group in all of China, something which could have been (and, in some respects, was) utilized by the CCP to keep the Communist movement going in the county. Still, many factors counterbalanced their numerical superiority, meaning that the peasant numbers could not be exploited by the CCP to the degree necessary to swing the tide in their favor. Thus, Mao Zedong, the CCP, and its leaders, having organized the Red Army after the Nanchang Uprising, continued fighting for the Communist cause, though the scale of their activities was nowhere near the one present in the early days of the United Front movement. For the next few years, the CCP was reduced to a guerilla fighting band, and the main stage was almost fully assumed by the KMT.

The situation was drastically different for the KMT. The left-wing Wuhan government, led by Wang Jingwei, soon decided to reconcile with Chiang Kai-shek and the rest of the KMT at Nanjing. Several reasons explain this move. Mainly, the leftist KMT government of Wuhan realized it had lost much of its influence and power with the departure of the Communists. Indeed, the CCP had always brought a lot of funding and military support with them thanks to their Soviet friends, but without them, the KMT members at Wuhan were nowhere near strong enough to continue the revolutionary movement by themselves. This became clear after the Nanchang Uprising when the Communists came very close to victory. Wang Jingwei and his supporters in Wuhan briefly engaged in conflict with the Nanjing government of Chiang Kai-shek, with Wang even forcing Chiang to resign as president of the party soon after the Nanchang Uprising in September 1927. However, Chiang Kai-shek still had the support of the NRA, which he had personally led during the Northern Expedition, giving him influence that was basically gone with his resignation. This, paired with increased Communist revolts throughout the KMT-controlled provinces, eventually forced the Wuhan government to disband itself, reuniting with the government in Nanjing in September of 1927. Wang Jingwei and several prominent anti-Chiang members of the KMT refused to rejoin, fleeing the country.

Wang Jingwei.
*https://commons.wikimedia.org/wiki/File:%E6%B1%AA%E7%B2%BE%E8%A1%9B%
E7%85%A7%E7%89%87.jpg*

Political maneuvering in the months following the reconciliation between the Wuhan and the Nanjing governments in late 1927 eventually concluded with Chiang Kai-shek's return. It was important that the revolutionaries still pursued their mission of reconquering and reunifying all of China, and many KMT members, especially the younger ones who had joined the party during the Northern Expedition, saw Chiang Kai-shek as the best person to lead them to their goal. Chiang reassumed command of the fractured NRA troops on January 1, 1928, and began planning the second phase of the Northern Expedition, which envisioned finishing the task the revolutionaries had started a few years back.

On his way to reunification, however, Chiang Kai-shek was constantly confronted with warlords with sizeable armies that governed over large territories in different Chinese provinces. As it soon became clear, the NRA general adopted a symbiotic relationship with the warlords, absorbing them into the NRA as he moved north. He made friends with different powerful warlords, promising them large degrees of autonomy in exchange for their support of the revolutionary cause. By mid-1928, the National

Revolutionary Army thus was not the only force involved in the second phase of the Northern Expedition. In addition to the core that had been there since the very beginning of the movement, there were several warlord armies nominally under the leadership of Chiang Kai-shek (but, in reality, acting largely on their own for the same cause). Yan Xishan, the warlord of the Shanxi province, and Feng Yuxiang, the leader and warlord of the Anhui clique, were two of the most prominent warlords who joined Chiang Kai-shek and were granted gracious concessions by the NRA commander, who was re-elected president of the KMT in October 1928.

The expedition thus continued to undermine the Beiyang government, which was only tightly in control of the capital and had assembled the National Pacification Army (NPA) to counter the revolutionary movement. The structure of the NPA was similar to that of the NRA, comprised of multiple pro-Beiyang warlords who were promised great rewards for fighting for the government. However, the multi-pronged NRA offensive proved too difficult for the Beiyang government to deal with. Various contingents of the revolutionary forces would attack at different points, often breaking the resistance and pushing the loyalists back from the northern bank of the Yangzi River to Zhengzhou and Xuzhou. Then, the revolutionaries moved into Shandong, still under Japanese occupation. Although Chiang Kai-shek tried to negotiate a peaceful withdrawal of Japanese forces from the city of Jinan, the capital of Shandong, a disagreement broke out between the Japanese and the NRA troops inside the city, resulting in the killing of about 16 Japanese civilians in May 1928. In response, the Japanese sent the 6th division of the Imperial Army to Jinan, driving the NRA out of the province and killing more than 6,000 Chinese soldiers and civilians. The Jinan Incident was a defeat for Chiang Kai-shek and the NRA, and the Shandong province remained under Japanese control for another year.

Still, even this could not kill the nationalist drive of the revolutionaries. With the warlords on his side, Chiang Kai-shek was confident that victory was close. Shandong was an adjacent province to Beijing, meaning the NRA was closing in on the Beiyang. While the main NRA army and Feng Yuxiang's contingent were temporarily held off by the NPA while trying to converge on the capital, the third revolutionary army under Yan Xishan swept in from Shanxi to capture the pivotal Nankou (Juyong Pass) in late May, essentially cutting off the NPA from many of the railway lines. This, as well as growing pressure from Japan that any fighting in Japanese-controlled territories would result in a full-scale invasion, demoralized the Beiyang troops, and the NRA forces reached Beijing in early June without much resistance. Incidentally, it was Yan Xishan's forces who took the city for the revolutionaries, while Chiang Kai-shek and the rest of the NRA forces arrived several days later to reinforce. The capture of Beijing was followed by a series of surrenders from NPA generals, which basically guaranteed the revolutionaries' victory. The formal end to the Northern Expedition came in December 1928, when the KMT forces invaded and defeated the resisting forces in Manchuria, reuniting China and starting ten years of unrivaled KMT dominance deemed the Nanjing Decade.

The Nationalist Era

Upon assuming power in Beijing, the KMT, officially led by Chiang Kai-shek from October 1928, began consolidating its control over the country, still largely divided among different provincial warlords who enjoyed large degrees of autonomy. In fact, as the nationalists advanced further north from their original base in Guangzhou, their grip over the conquered provinces was slowly slipping away, with local leaders emerging to defy KMT dominance in their respective areas. Whether or not the provincial unrest had resulted from Communist activities or anti-KMT sentiment varied from province to province. Essentially, in the early days of the revolutionaries' success, the power held by Chiang Kai-shek and the KMT was concentrated in the lower Yangzi Valley, in the central-eastern part of the country around the cities of Nanjing and Shanghai. This region was the wealthiest and the most advanced in the whole country, giving the KMT just enough influence to stay at the top, although not enabling him to declare complete power over the Chinese warlords.

All of China was also suffering from the problems that had been largely dealt with in other industrialized countries several decades before. Mainly, the country was heavily disconnected, having no real infrastructural and communication networks to connect its vast lands with each other. This made it difficult for the central government to raise taxes from more rural provinces; it relied on the local provincial gentry to keep control. State bureaucracy was almost nonexistent in these places, only managing to cover big cities. Even the relationships with the different pro-KMT warlords were very complicated: Yan Xishan, whose army had been fighting with Chiang Kai-shek and had captured Beijing, eventually rebelled against the KMT and was suppressed after a bloody war. Smaller-scale regional conflicts were ongoing throughout the Nanjing Decade, propagated in part by the Communists and in part by the lack of control over these lands.

Still, the nationalist government under Chiang Kai-shek did start to address at least some of the problems the country faced. The lack of infrastructure plagued China's development the most, so the KMT devoted a lot of funds to building new roads and railways, followed by telegraph lines. The growth of local industries and production resulted in subtle economic benefits. Simultaneously, negotiations with the Western powers who still held interests in China's ports returned at least partial control over the country's trade tariff and customs services to the central government. At first glance, it looked as if China was finally emerging as a united nation-state—a feat that had been achieved by all the major powers in the world throughout the past hundred years. A functioning nation-state, however, needed unity, stability, and the will of the people. And in the long run, it also required the transformation of the country's political system from a one-party authoritarian rule to a liberal democracy.

In this regard, the nationalist government did not make quite as much progress. The KMT, which had been created to promote the three principles of Sun Yat-sen—nationalism, democracy, and the welfare of the people—was almost completely forgotten. The nationalistic element was reflected in the return to Confucian ideas, heavily promoted by Chiang Kai-shek himself, who, along with the rest of the party, believed that the Chinese people were not ready to accept democracy as a ruling system. In fact, the nationalists were emerging much closer to the far-right systems in Europe in the 1930s, with Chiang Kai-shek even having German advisors in his army and administration. The regime did not reach the point of racial segregation and discrimination, of course, but the partial return to strict traditional Confucianism was slowly evaporating the democratic progress the country had made since the late 1890s. It seemed as if Chiang Kai-shek was trying to become a sort of enlightened despot who would bring about great change and innovation in the country in exchange for a partially free society. He believed that a nation's citizens should serve the interests of the state and that a good citizen did not question the government's authority and intentions since they were always what was best for the nation. However, as already outlined, China could hardly be called a unified state due to all the provincial and regional divisions that caused a heavily decentralized system.

As historians have identified, Chiang Kai-shek's biggest problem was that he did not fully identify with any ideology and therefore lacked support from any distinct group. For example, the sort of traditional, Confucian, pseudo-democratic, nationalist (call it whatever you will) regime he pursued was not really appealing to the civilian masses, and the support he accumulated came mostly from those affiliated with the party. A group of people who perhaps liked the approach of Chiang Kai-shek the most was the urban middle class, which made up only a small minority of the entire population. Even with them, getting across a political message from the government was still difficult due to the obscure tendencies of the KMT leader. Within the party and the army, most high-ranking officials were personally related to Chiang Kai-shek, meaning that he was surrounded, in many cases, by people who were not necessarily the best at their jobs.

The lack of coordination regarding ideology became increasingly clear as the Communist movement restarted its activities after going underground in late 1927. Common people largely supported a stable central government and the modernization of the country but were far less attracted to the KMT and Chiang Kai-shek. The lower classes had found their voice during the revolutionary movement in the CCP, which had a clearly-defined political, social, and economic agenda that seemed beneficial for them. The KMT, in comparison, never quite connected to the masses to the extent of the CCP, although its original intent and goals had been noble and good-willed. The CCP had established far better contact with the people during the days of the United Front, while the KMT had cut off this contact when it split from the Communists.

CCP Reborn

Throughout all this time, as the KMT and Chiang Kai-shek were trying to establish some degree of central control over the country, the routed CCP groups continued their actions, though not to the same extent as before the split with the KMT. After the failed uprisings to take the major cities of central and southern China, the Communists, as we already mentioned, were forced out of the mainstream political spectrum. The CCP leaders, Mao Zedong among them, were put in quite a challenging situation: nearly all progress the party had made on the political stage was backtracked, and if it did not act decisively very soon, the appeal of Communism among the masses might also fade away. Crucially, the CCP no longer had support from Moscow, as Stalin had decided to focus on domestic action rather than promote a global Communist revolution. This meant that the "Red Army," which had been established during the Nanchang Uprising, had nowhere near the strength and experience of local warlord forces, let alone the nationalist army under Chiang Kai-shek. It was made up of criminals and bandits, most of whom were only lately familiarized with the Communist cause and had largely concerned themselves with regular banditry before it. The CCP had only gotten lucky because the central government could not further crack down on the Communists after the capture of Beijing. Had Chiang Kai-shek had a competent hold over the country, it is very possible the Communist movement would have been completely suppressed by the central government.

This chaotic situation gave an advantage to the less-powerful CCP, as Mao Zedong was able to come together with another CCP leader and former army commander, Zhu De. Joining their forces, the Communists managed to take over some land from 1928 to 1931 in the southeastern part of the country, in the provinces of Jiangxi and Fujian. This territory, which would soon come under the total control of the CCP, would soon be named the "Chinese Soviet Republic," also known as the Jiangxi-Fujian Soviet. Zhu De was made the supreme commander-in-chief of the Red Army, while Mao kept his senior status in the party and was its effective leader.

Together, the two sought to revive the Communist drive among the local peasant and worker populations, trying to reach the lower classes in rural areas who were unavailable to the central government when most previous party leaders had fled the country after the failure to undermine KMT dominance.

What made the actions of Mao and the CCP different from other Marxist movements until this point was their shift of focus to the peasants as the drivers of the revolution instead of the working class. This principle diverged from the Marxist doctrine, as Marx had outlined that the proletariat—the group of people destined to emerge from the oppression of the bourgeoisie—would be made up of the working class, who had been ruthlessly exploited throughout history by the upper classes. In the case of China, however, at least after the dissolution of the United Front, the CCP encouraged the mobilization of the peasants as the main force for revolution, assimilating them with the working classes—the traditional Marxist revolutionaries. Of course, at the beginning of their activities, the Chinese Communists had risen to prominence thanks to the workers they indoctrinated with Marxist ideas. But the situation in the 1930s was far more complicated.

Not only had the CCP lost most of its influence and reach with the workers, reduced to a small and concentrated movement in the countryside, but a Communist revolution led by peasants had never been perceived possible, let alone tried (albeit they only had the small sample size of one successful Communist revolution). The Marxist struggle of the classes was traditionally between the poor and the rich or workers and the bourgeoisie, respectively. Peasants held varying degrees of wealth in China to encourage them to strive for class equality, and richer peasants sometimes employed poorer peasants to work for them. In addition, a peasant Communist revolution was further inconceivable for many traditional Communists, especially in Russia, since Stalin himself was cracking down on the richer "kulak" peasants inside the Soviet Union, deeming them enemies of the state. The true strength of Russian Communism lay in urban areas, where the majority of the working class was concentrated, and seeing Mao rely on peasants for an eventual revolution was simply unorthodox for many Communists.

This divergence from the traditional Marxist doctrine, along with the fact that the rural populations of China had virtually no experience with democratic, industrial, or capitalistic institutions and were hierarchical among themselves, made applying the Marxist doctrine trickier. Still, Mao and the CCP's solution to these problems was to adapt the revolution's goal—which was, in theory, a full-on classless society. Instead of advocating for this type of system, which would have drastically differed from what the peasant populations had been used to for centuries, Mao proposed gradual land reform: a basic redistribution from the rich to the poor. This, unsurprisingly, won the hearts of many poorer peasants who were familiar with extreme living conditions and starvation in their current lives. The Land Law of the Chinese Revolutionary Military Council, passed in 1930, appealed to many: if one person owned more land than he needed, his lands would be redistributed to the point that other people who practically owned nothing received some benefits. The land reform was vastly successful in the territories controlled by the CCP, and thousands of peasants saw the Communists as their saviors. Many even voluntarily enlisted in the Red Army, gradually shifting the balance from thieves and ex-criminals to people who cared about the party's success. Crucially, the land reform even found support among the higher-ranking peasants and some landowners, who decided to adapt to their "new rulers" instead of opposing them. In a decentralized country such as China, where parts of the population were completely disconnected from each other, locals believed that it would be better for them to accept the rule imposed by the CCP rather than protest in the name of the central government, not the least because the central government cared little about what was going on in Beijing and weren't concerned with its citizens' day-to-day lives.

Thus, as far as the CCP was concerned, the land reform was a partial success, but a success nevertheless, giving the party a boost of confidence to continue its actions, now almost fully independent from Comintern support. It seemed that the switch of focus from the working class to the peasants was a viable strategy that was leading, in a way, to a healthier revolutionary process than what had transpired in Russia. Lenin and his supporters had virtually no experience running a government, let alone a whole economy, when they assumed power in the quick turn of events in 1917. Yes, the Communist revolution was complete, but the inexperienced Bolsheviks faced many challenges trying to make progress and implement good changes, which Lenin himself acknowledged in his writings.

Mao and the CCP, however, started ruling over a smaller, much more manageable territory and gained supporters from the masses who were true to the Communist cause (or at least heavily influenced by it). The rise of Communism in China after the dissolution of the United Front in 1927 became a gradual, step-by-step process—an unorthodox approach to the concept of the revolution, but still a hopeful and effective one. Mao and the other leaders of the movement would gain valuable experience during these times, which would come in handy later on down the line.

As we covered briefly, divergence from the "traditional" style of the Communist revolution to the one adopted by Mao was met with some resistance from the Communists in Russia. Technically speaking, the CCP had always been an organization that was a product of the Comintern, which had provided much material support and inspired the Communist movement to emerge in China. After the CCP's unsuccessful attempts to take over cities in the uprisings of 1927-1928, however, the cohesion between the Comintern and the party had been almost fully destroyed. Many CCP members had also abandoned the country after the failure of the uprisings and fled to Moscow, where they still nominally led the movement in China. Observing Mao's different approach to the revolution, many Communists in Moscow started criticizing the movement, despite its relative success given the state of the party and the country since the late 1920s.

Thus, by late 1931, as Moscow Communists noticed the small but steady growth of the Communists in China, they sent back a group of young Chinese Communists known as the "28 Bolsheviks." These youngsters had been educated and indoctrinated in Marxism and the revolution in Moscow at Sun Yat-sen University, which had been created in 1925 to honor the ties between the Chinese revolutionary leader and the Soviet Union. The 28 Bolsheviks were traditional and doctrinal in their approach to the concept of revolution (and Communism in general). They were sent from Moscow to reassume party leadership and divert the

Chinese Communist revolution back to the traditional ways.

It is not surprising that the 28 Bolsheviks came into conflict with Mao upon their arrival. Their inflexible views, a product of their education, simply did not fit the conditions of China. By that time, Mao's approach to the revolution was far more effective. He was willing to compromise a little on some of the "textbook" revolutionary details, such as a pure class struggle, for his adaptive policies, such as land redistribution. The 28 Bolsheviks, for example, saw richer peasants and small landowners as part of the oppressor bourgeois class and pushed for more extreme measures to achieve equality among all classes. They not only accused Mao of appeasing them to gain more power for himself but also believed the movement had lost its truly Communist origins and intentions and was being corrupted.

There were more differences in their military activities and strategy. Here, again, Mao favored guerilla tactics, avoiding head-to-head clashes with the KMT forces that were much more competent in the field than the Red Army. Mao believed (correctly) that the CCP could not afford such encounters and was sometimes even willing to give up previously Communist-controlled lands to the KMT forces and retreat until a good opportunity to counterattack arose. The 28 Bolsheviks considered this approach a cowardly manifestation of Mao's true personality, believing that temporarily giving up land harmed the future of the revolution.

Still, from 1930 to 1934, Chiang Kai-shek's KMT forces tried five times to end the Jiangxi Soviet by launching offensives known as "encirclement campaigns." KMT armies encroached on CCP positions in southeast China but were either outright repelled (thanks, in part, to the poor communication they had so far away from central command in Nanjing), or managed to achieve only minor victories, with the Communists managing to expel them from temporarily lost territories after a few weeks.

The most major engagement was the fifth encirclement, which took place in 1934 when Chiang Kai-shek adopted a new approach that proved to be rather effective. Instead of relying on numbers to meet the Communists in battle and rout them, the KMT forces methodically advanced on the Jiangxi holdings, laying siege to their territories in summer. The new strategy was more effective because it tried to strangle the Communists by cutting off their supply lines and slowly closing in on their armies.

The 28 Bolsheviks argued that the Red Army must defend the gains of the CCP, whose numbers were being stretched thin, making it easier for the KMT to break through—something that came true in early October. Following the KMT push, the Red Army was forced to orchestrate a massive retreat known as the Long March from Jiangxi, abandoning their positions to the scale not often seen in modern warfare.

The Long March was a pivotal point for the CCP. About 100,000 people, including party members, Red Army soldiers, and regular peasants and Communist supporters, endured an extremely difficult journey through the country for nearly a year. As the encirclement campaign closed in on the Communists' position, people soon realized they needed to abandon almost everything if they wanted to survive, as the KMT did not hesitate to outright execute Communist sympathizer peasants if they were found out. The CCP, retreating from the southern part of Jiangxi, first traveled west through Hunan and Guizhou, constantly chased by the KMT forces. From there, they pivoted north from the province of Yunnan into the mountainous regions of Sichuan and Gansu before finally arriving in the northern province of Shaanxi about a year after they departed from Jiangxi. Throughout the march, thousands of Communists joined the CCP due to the threat of the KMT, but few would endure the terrible journey that would be plagued with a myriad of issues. In October 1935, the CCP was allowed to settle down for a bit due to other developments we will cover later. A year of evasion had reduced the movement's numbers about ten times: no more than 10,000 Communists managed to survive the Long March. Those who did, however—the most veteran members, including Mao Zedong—would dominate the party and be instrumental in the rebirth of the Chinese Communist movement throughout the next ten years.

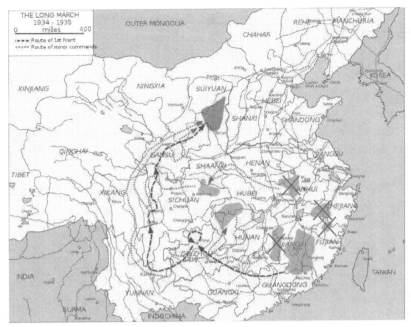

A map of the Long March.

The Long March was also very important in that Mao emerged as the official leader of the CCP. In January 1935, he was named the chairman of the Politburo, making him the effective leader of both the party and the army. Despite this, Mao did not exclude others from party leadership, realizing that he could not lead such a large movement by himself, especially in such desperate times. Although he was the most important member who supervised almost all party decisions, other Communists, such as Zhu De, Den Xiaoping, Lin Biao, and Liu Shaoqi, also ran the party and its activities. The cooperation and trust these individuals would accumulate during the Long March would help the CCP achieve its goals in the future. The resilience demonstrated by the Communists during the march also reassured many of the revolutionary drive largely present among the people. Of course, Mao's amiable relations with the rest of the prominent party members would only last until the 1950s and 60s, when he assumed totalitarian control over the country. But that hardly downplays the cooperation that was present among the revolutionaries during the hardest times.

Also, crucially, many historians have recognized that the CCP had adapted to the country's changing political landscape during the Long March and had emerged as both a nationalist organization and a Communist movement. With Mao as its leader, a man who had demonstrated that diverging from traditional Marxist doctrines worked for the sake of the revolution, the CCP's main goal was the unification and the socio-economic development of the Chinese nation, alongside the eventual implementation of a Marxist regime. In these regards, one could say that the CCP was more nationalistic than the KMT—the nationalist party at the head of the country. Chiang Kai-shek and his subordinates were busy pursuing their own interests after assuming power and seldom cared for the country's overall transformation from a backwards state to a powerful entity that could utilize its resources to achieve international success and recognition. While it is true that the nationalist government promoted projects to increase connectivity and production, the reforms were relatively small-scale, troubled by warlord separatists who hindered any meaningful progress. Chiang Kai-shek's approach was one of appeasement and cooperation, which did not do the country any good. The CCP, with Mao as its leader, on the other hand, focused more on strengthening the nation by promoting the rights and freedoms of the poor, who constituted the majority of the population.

Second United Front

Meanwhile, China found itself in another political crisis with the Japanese. Japan had retained its hostility and interest in China even as other powers, such as France and Great Britain, had given up much of the privileges they once held in the country's port cities. The Japanese encroachment on China and its influence on Chinese domestic affairs had been increasing ever since Japan's militarization campaigns, which had made the nation perhaps the most powerful in all of Asia. The Japanese had occupied the Liaodong Peninsula since the 1920s and were heavily interested in the far northeastern Chinese province of Manchuria. Manchuria, one of the largest and the most remote regions, had long been a point of contention between the Chinese, Japanese, and even the Russians due to its ports and natural resources. Zhang Zuolin, the Manchurian warlord who had fought against the United Front during the Northern Expedition, was on relatively friendly terms with the Japanese, allowing them to pursue their interests in Manchuria in exchange for financial support. However, with the "successful" revolution of Chiang Kai-shek and the defeat and subsequent assassination of Zhang Zuolin, the Japanese became concerned that the new nationalist government might try to drive them out of Manchuria.

These developments also coincided with the reignition of militarism and nationalism in Japan, as the Great Depression had decimated the country's economy. Thus, many army officers, who were increasingly aggressive in their approach to foreign relations, pushed for the invasion of Manchuria, which they believed would be a reassertion of Japanese dominance in the region. They also knew that the Chinese nationalist government in Nanjing would be unable to properly respond, especially as Chiang Kai-shek was not particularly hostile towards the Japanese even though the rest of the country believed Japan was a natural enemy. These officers presented their plans to high command, but after getting rejected, decided to stage an explosion at the Japanese-controlled South Manchuria Railway in September of 1931. The Japanese then blamed the act on the Chinese, giving them a justification to invade the province and take it for themselves. In a quick war that lasted for not more than five months, the Japanese Imperial Army, much more competent and professional, defeated the Manchurian forces of Zhang Xueliang—the new warlord of the province—and took over Manchuria in a breeze.

Chiang Kai-shek's response to the Japanese invasion was nonconfrontational, to say the least. Although the leader of the nationalist government knew that the loss of the province was not good, he believed that the Communists were a far worse threat than the Japanese. After Zhang Xueliang was forced to withdraw from Manchuria during the invasion of 1931, Chiang Kai-shek made him commander of the Chinese Northeastern Army in 1936 and tasked him with dealing with the Communists who had completed their Long March and had settled in Shaanxi. Zhang Xueliang, leading the KMT forces against the Red Army, however, would not manage to achieve anything significant for the nationalists. On the contrary, he became a sympathizer with the CCP who pushed for Chinese unity against a common enemy in the form of imperialist Japan.

Wanting to retake Manchuria and confident that the only possible way was cooperation between the CCP and the KMT, Zhang Xueliang kidnapped Chiang Kai-shek in the city of Xi'an in December of 1936. He then brought the nationalist leader to the CCP, who agreed to release Chiang Kai-shek (although they saw him as a threat, just like Japan) in exchange for an anti-Japanese coalition between the two parties. The KMT was forced to agree, as it essentially could not continue without Chiang, leading to the formation of what is known as the Second United Front. The KMT and the CCP were allies once again, united against the looming threat of a foreign enemy nearly a decade after their first alliance.

Mao and Chiang during the Second United Front days, 1945.
https://commons.wikimedia.org/wiki/File:1945_Mao_and_Chiang.jpg

Chiang Kai-shek was still the country's leader, and the Communists recognized the Nanjing government as legitimate. The CCP was not allowed to join the government, although it was given a degree of autonomy in its affairs in Shaanxi, and KMT forces stopped their crackdown on the Communists. In addition, the Red Army, now nominally under the command of Chiang Kai-shek but still largely operating as a separate force, was incorporated as the Eighth Route Army of China, and other Communist contingents around the country were also organized into forces of their own.

Seeing this, the Soviets also briefly resumed their relations with the Chinese and provided them with military and financial aid. Thus, the Second United Front was ready to lead the country out of a crisis once more, although both sides perhaps knew that their new alliance was doomed to eventually fail like their old one.

Chapter Five – China at War

The Second Sino-Japanese War

In the early 1930s, after the invasion of Manchuria and the establishment of a puppet state named Manchukuo, the Japanese continued to aggressively force their hand in different Chinese lands. Adding insult to injury, they installed the final Qing leader— Puyi—as the leader of Manchukuo, which was received hostilely by the Chinese population. Then, the Japanese asserted that they were the main actors in Chinese politics, saying that nothing major would happen without their consent. In this political climate, Chiang Kai-shek had been reluctant to oppose the Japanese, aware that he simply did not have the means to resist the Japanese army. He was also more concerned with the Communist movement during this time, sending army after army to encircle the Communists at Jiangxi and eventually forcing them to retreat on the Long March. However, since late 1936, after a forced coalition with the CCP, Chiang Kai-shek had made it clear that the intentions of the nationalist government at Nanjing were also hostile towards the Japanese. Thus, after years of crawling occupation, intimidation, coercion, and threats, the Japanese finally decided to launch a full-scale invasion of China in July 1937 after an incident between the countries' soldiers at the Marco Polo Bridge resulted in armed confrontation.

With the breakout of war, many regional leaders and political forces within the country soon rallied to the support of the Second

United Front. Everyone agreed that the Japanese were a common, foreign threat—enough of an incentive to unite. Still, the war machine of ultra-nationalist Japan proved too difficult to handle, even if the Chinese far outnumbered the enemy. As the invasion unfolded, Japanese offensives emerged from Manchuria and the sea, with the imperial forces managing to take most major Chinese port cities in the first year and a half of fighting. Lower Yangzi, where most of the wealth and power of nationalist China had been concentrated, was especially prone to a naval invasion, and the Japanese quickly gained decisive victories over the KMT armies in Shanghai, Nanjing, and Wuhan by October 1938. The attack also came to southern China from the island of Taiwan, then under Japanese control, and the Chinese soon lost Hong Kong and surrounding areas to the enemy. The biggest difference was that the Japanese soldiers were highly trained and well-equipped, whereas the Second United Front suffered from terrible discipline, a shortage of supplies and coordination, and a lack of competent command. The loss of such important cities, including the nationalist capital of Nanjing, forced the government to flee west, relocating far away from the center of the conflict in Chongqing.

However, by early 1939, the Second Sino-Japanese War came to a stalemate. After an extremely successful initial offensive campaign, Japan took over the most important cities of China, most of which were concentrated in the eastern part of the country, and maintained its occupation by establishing a permanent military presence. Still, as the Chinese government and forces had retreated to the west and settled in Chongqing, the Japanese could not pursue them that far to force their surrender. The truth was that China was simply too big for Japan to completely occupy, let alone continue to effectively hold. Japanese holdings stretched somewhat thin along the coast, but that was basically it. Going deep inland was dangerous for Japan, as the troops would be prone to guerilla attacks by Chinese soldiers. The Japanese strategy had been a quick invasion, believing that seizing the enemy's capital would mean its surrender. The case was, however, much different even though the Chinese government had lost most of its army and means of continuing the war effort. Even in the occupied territories, wherever Japan had the manpower to impose its rule, local populations were rarely keen on foreign invaders and seldom cooperated. Thus, after the initial wave of invasion and the retreat of the Chinese government, Japanese advancements in China temporarily stopped.

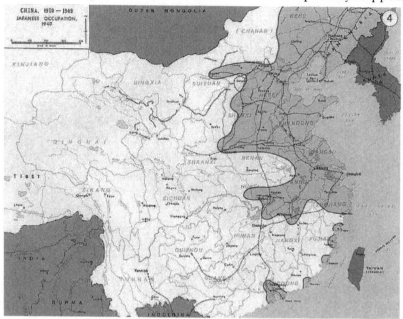

Japanese occupation of China.
https://commons.wikimedia.org/wiki/File:Japanese_Occupation_-_Map.jpg

In their approach to the occupied, the Japanese were as ruthless as it gets. They viewed the Chinese as their natural enemies and subordinates—something that can be attributed to the prominence of the far-right nationalist regime and ideology, obviously not only present in Japan at the time. As they took over territories, the Japanese rarely took prisoners. They executed the large majority of forces they captured and decimated even peaceful civilian populations. Infamously, the most prevalent case of Japanese war crimes during their invasion of China is the Nanjing Massacre, where an estimated 300,000 soldiers and civilians were ruthlessly killed by the occupying forces. Rape, torture, and other terrible crimes were also common during the war, resulting in one of the most horrifying conflicts of the 20th century.

World War 2

At the outbreak of World War 2, the two warring countries had essentially entered a stalemate: neither one was able to fully force the other to surrender. By 1940, as the German invasion of France left French possessions in Indochina vulnerable, Japan was able to expand in the region and gain access to the southern part of China through Indochina. The Japanese had essentially created a ring of occupation on the border of China, having occupied all the major cities and routes that could have been used by the Chinese government to continue the war effort. As for the Chinese, the retreat to Chongqing proved to be a bittersweet decision. Although the Sichuan Mountains provided a very difficult natural barrier between the fleeing Chinese national government and the invaders, the underdeveloped provinces of Western China provided few resources for the KMT to effectively fight off the Japanese. In fact, most of the fighting after the initial wave of the Japanese invasion was decentralized, with smaller, mostly Communist forces employing guerilla tactics against the Japanese. These forces were scattered around the country and, despite being nowhere near as strong as the Japanese troops, managed to stall the conflict while the main Chinese contingents fled west with the government.

Japan's ties with Nazi Germany during the war meant that nationalist China and the Allies were natural partners. For the Europeans, pushing back the Japanese would have strategic and symbolic importance—signaling that fascism could be overcome. Thus, the Allies constantly tried to provide supplies and resources to the "exiled" Chinese government in Chongqing, which was in a very tough situation. The fight for China was especially amplified after the Japanese attack on Pearl Harbor in December 1941 and the entry of the United States into the war on the side of the Allies. Following the attack, Japan invaded the Philippines, Indonesia, Malaya, and Burma, taking over lands rich with vital resources like oil and rubber while also cutting off a reliable Allied supply route to China. Japan's quick expansion and domination of the Pacific and southern Asia posed a big threat to the Allies, and the US strategy to fight against them involved a great deal of help from the Chinese government.

General Joseph Stillwell would be the commander-in-chief of the US operations in Asia, and he made contact with Chiang Kai-shek's government in Chongqing shortly after his country entered the war. Stillwell proposed that Chiang mobilize whatever forces he had to coordinate a joint attack on the Japanese, something which was refused by the KMT leader, who was reluctant to aid the Americans. Chiang Kai-shek's justification, other than his general distrust towards foreigners and unwillingness to spend his limited resources, was that his men were untrained and ill-equipped, and he showed little enthusiasm to show any support to the Americans during the war. He deeply believed that the US could beat Japan without his help and that he would need whatever resources—arms, munitions, men—he could gather after the war when an eventual power vacuum would demand it. This led to a lack of trust between Chiang Kai-shek and Stillwell, and the two's relations heavily deteriorated throughout the war, with the Chinese leader even refusing to accept direct training of his troops by the American generals.

Eventually, Stillwell was forced to change his strategy and instead approached the Communists who were still putting up a fight in Northern China. In fact, the Communist base of operations in the far northern Shaanxi region, centering on the city of Yan'an, was hardly touched by the Japanese, who did not dare to venture that far due to the Communist guerilla resistance prominent in the area. After the retreat of the KMT to Chongqing, the CCP had grown its range of activities in Northern China, with much more people emerging as supporters of the Communist cause than before. The Communists' main problem was that they lacked military equipment sufficient for their men—something that could be aptly provided by the United States. Mao Zedong was more than happy for the cooperation between his party and the US. US support, if established, would reduce the CCP's heavy dependence on the Soviet Union (which was in a rather precarious situation, with him getting similar aid from the US) and provide means for further resistance and the flourishing of the revolution after the end of the war. In July of 1944, after General Stillwell was replaced by General Wedemeyer, a secret United States Observation Group, also called the Dixie Mission, made contact with the CCP in Yan'an despite Chiang Kai-shek's insistence. The Americans and the Chinese Communists struck a deal, smuggling hundreds of tons of supplies for the Communists in Shaanxi. This boosted the CCP morale and put further pressure on the Japanese, as the re-armed Communists managed to put up a better fight during the guerilla engagements.

However, in hindsight, it was not the American aid to the CCP that won the Allies the war against the Japanese in China. Nor was it the little support the superpower had given to the KMT. Pragmatically speaking, the CCP was never a desirable option for the US, as American sentiment was still largely anti-Communist despite the alliance between the Soviet Union and the US during the war. In the eyes of the American public, Chiang Kai-shek had been built up as the true leader of China and was very popular due to his American-educated wife. The couple even posed with General Stillwell for a photo that spread throughout the country. Still, the public did not know that behind the happy, smiling faces of those pictured in the photograph, there lay a massive wedge between Chiang and Stillwell and that, actually, the KMT had missed an opportunity to truly increase its strength both during and after the war. The support the US gave to the CCP did little to swing the conflict's tides in favor of the Chinese on the continent, although fighting never truly stopped. What eventually forced the Japanese to surrender a little more than a year after the Dixie Mission were the two atomic bombs dropped on Hiroshima and Nagasaki in August of 1945, resulting in destruction and death on a level previously unseen.

The Civil War Resumes

It is not an overstatement to say that the sudden surrender of Japan in August came as a genuine surprise to everyone, including the United States. Before using the atomic bomb, the US had even negotiated a deal with the Soviets that called for Stalin to declare war on Japan to help with its defeat. Stalin did declare war on August 8, two days after the first bomb was a "success" at Hiroshima, and Soviet troops invaded and occupied Manchuria without much resistance. After the second bomb was dropped on Nagasaki a day later, Japanese morale was almost completely destroyed, resulting in an unconditional capitulation to the Allies a few days later. This rather abrupt ending to imperialist Japan and its ability to wage war meant that China was basically up for grabs, but whether the Communists or the KMT would emerge as the dominant force was still in question.

The months following the Japanese surrender were chaotic, to say the least. The two Chinese forces had jointly declared on August

28 that they would continue peaceful cooperation and aim for the democratic development and unification of China, but that was hardly the case. In reality, both the CCP and the KMT hurried to reclaim their control in the Japanese-occupied Chinese cities and exclude the other. Encounters between their troops sometimes even resulted in armed confrontations, as the Communists accused the nationalists of inaction and cowardice during the war, while the nationalist forces despised the Communist cause more than they despised the Japanese.

What made matters even more complicated was the involvement and interests of the US and the Soviet Union in post-war China. President Truman, who continued President Roosevelt's approach, believed that a non-Communist China was necessary to contain the spread of Communism from its base in the USSR. Thus, immediately following the end of the war, the US adopted several pro-KMT measures that helped ameliorate Chiang Kai-shek's position in the country. The Marshall Mission, headed by General George C. Marshall, envisioned a peaceful transition to a functioning central government. This included agreements signed by both parties in early 1946, calling for steps such as reducing the overall number of military divisions within the CCP and the KMT. However, the CCP was only allowed to retain 18 divisions to the KMT's 90. It is not difficult to grasp that the Marshall Mission favored the nationalists far more than the Communists.

Although the KMT had secured the most valuable Chinese cities, the CCP still had a very strong presence in the countryside, with most of the people overwhelmingly on its side. Chiang Kai-shek knew the Communists posed the biggest threat to him and wanted to strike before they could grow their movement stronger, potentially with help from their Soviet friends (although Stalin was more focused on rebuilding his own country than helping the CCP at that point). Thus, whenever the opportunity presented itself, KMT forces continued to advance in heavily disputed areas, not afraid to clash with the CCP. The struggle between the two Chinese factions became especially apparent in Manchuria, where the retreat of occupying Soviet troops resulted in a series of armed confrontations between the CCP and the KMT and the province's essential split by mid-1946. By late 1946, the KMT troops were spread thin, stationed around the country in most of the big cities, while the Communists were trying to reorganize and recalibrate their plans.

These developments were accompanied by a series of failed agreements between the two sides, mediated by the US, which realized that the support it had given to Chiang Kai-shek was being blatantly exploited by the KMT to suppress the growth of the CCP. The US wanted a stable, anti-Communist China as a future ally against the Soviet Union, but the situation in the country by the end of 1946 was nowhere near anti-Communist, let alone stable. The fact that Chiang Kai-shek had managed to occupy most of the urban areas of the country did not exactly mean that the Communists were not strong. In fact, all this time they had actively pursued their political activities, motivating hundreds of thousands of people to join their revolutionary cause, which seemed as relevant as ever.

The the CCP's main instrument that was highly influential throughout the war was the return to a more radical land reform that targeted landlords and peasants at the top of the hierarchy and advocated for equality among all classes. This won the CCP much support from the poor peasants who dominated the Chinese countryside, resulting in the Communist army almost tripling in size by late 1946. In the rural areas controlled by the CCP, Communist leaders pushed for a very extreme policy against the rich, forcing the land holdings, tools, animals, and other possessions to be equally distributed among the people—an appealing policy for literally millions of Chinese who had lived in extreme poverty throughout their lives. Peasants flocked to support the CCP and were often granted senior positions inside the party thanks to their zeal and determination for a successful revolution. The CCP was not afraid to call out and punish local leaders who were found guilty of exercising their powers over the less privileged members of society.

China had never been remotely egalitarian. So, although its sudden transformation to a Communist state had proven to be impossible, the terrible mistakes of the KMT government and the public distrust towards Chiang Kai-shek had strengthened the Communist movement, at least to the point where it equaled the nationalists in power. The "liberated" parts of the country—as the

Communists called the areas they took over —provided a stern resistance to any KMT activities and emerged as regional centers of the movement throughout the country. This, paired with the fact that the United States (perhaps the main supporter of the nationalist government) was retracting much of its support in light of recent exploitation by Chiang Kai-shek, essentially meant that the triumph of the Communists was only a matter of time—something Chiang Kai-shek himself had recognized, as from the very beginning he had adopted an aggressive policy to root out Communism before it could get strong.

Communist Victory

Chiang Kai-shek's intention to end the civil war before it could break out eventually came to bite the nationalist leader in the back. Yes, KMT forces were the first to occupy major city centers after the Japanese withdrawal, but this only weakened the cohesion of the army at his disposal. The nationalist soldiers were untrained, ill-equipped, and demotivated, not quite knowing what they were fighting against. The right-wing KMT members in Chiang Kai-shek's factions had told them that Communism was the cancer of China, but their day-to-day experiences had proven otherwise. It was hard to ignore the widespread support for the CCP throughout the country, mostly in rural areas that were overwhelmingly in favor of the Communists. Thanks to this support, the KMT troops were never quite able to undermine the CCP presence and could not achieve significant military success against their enemies.

Since early 1947, Chiang Kai-shek had adopted an even more aggressive policy, ordering hundreds of thousands of KMT forces to march into northern China—the main base of operations for the Communists—a decision that ultimately brought only symbolic victories for the nationalists. The de-facto Communist capital of Yan'an was taken in March by the KMT, but it had been evacuated by the CCP days before the arrival of KMT forces. The Communists, reorganizing their forces into the People's Liberation Army (PLA), launched a series of counteroffensives to the aggressive pushes of the KMT. By the middle of 1947, as the KMT forces tried to drive out the Communists from Manchuria, it was becoming apparent that the nationalists were losing their zeal and drive while the Communists were gaining more direct and indirect power. For example, in Manchuria, the advantage held by the KMT was undermined by the functioning military equipment left to the PLA by the retreating Russians. With the North China Plain stretching over thousands of miles of countryside, the KMT stood no chance of dealing a severe blow to the CCP positions.

As the KMT forces diverged on the CCP positions from north and south, the PLA fled to the plains, drawing the inexperienced nationalists into a trap. Nationalist forces were stretched thin, trying to maintain a permanent presence in key cities but also lacking control over communication channels between them, rendering their efforts useless. From the autumn of 1948, the CCP counteroffensives bore fruit as they circled and destroyed large parts of KMT forces during the Liaoshen Campaign. By early November, the CCP had eliminated KMT resistance in the Northeast (Manchuria), including the major cities of Changchun, Jinzhou, and Shenyang. During this campaign, the KMT forces increasingly changed sides and joined the PLA, unwilling to continue endless fighting in tough conditions. The victory of the Liaoshen Campaign directly translated into the CCP victory during the Huaihai Campaign, in which the PLA marched south from their newly-acquired territories in the north and took control of Central China. From November 1948 to January 1949, the PLA defeated KMT forces one by one north of the Yangzi River. Seizing more land, KMT equipment, and leftover supplies, with hundreds of thousands of nationalists falling prisoner or straight-up switching sides, the PLA swept through Central China in one of the most decisive campaigns the country had ever seen, inflicting an estimated number of more than 500,000 casualties.

Meanwhile, as the two sides fiercely battled it out, it was becoming apparent that those suffering the most were ordinary folk whose lives had been deeply affected by the ongoing conflict. A roaring financial crisis in the country mostly hurt the lower and middle classes. Inflation soared high as the government's only response to national expenditure was printing more money. The wartime regime imposed by Chiang Kai-shek was catastrophic for the masses, something that further cut public support for the nationalists and incentivized the people to declare their support for the Communist cause.

In early 1949, Chiang Kai-shek realized that the war was not exactly going in his favor, with the KMT losing more and more ground every day. To avoid a disastrous defeat in the civil war that had spanned two decades, he proposed that peace be mediated by the Soviet Union, United Kingdom, United States, and France. Mao and the CCP followed up this proposal by clarifying that they would be open to peace negotiations if certain demands were met by the KMT. First, they demanded the abolition of the 1946 constitution preemptively drafted by the KMT and the dissolution of the current government. Then, the Communists wanted the prosecution and punishment of a list of "war criminals," including Chiang Kai-shek. Next, the CCP proposed the creation of a new coalition government with the nationalists, excluding the radical right-wing faction of Chiang Kai-shek. Finally, the Communists called for the confiscation of property from the oppressive government members in the capital and its redistribution to the poor, the introduction of a nationwide land reform, and the complete reorganization of the KMT army. To avoid full humiliation in the face of imminent defeat as the CCP's demands were presented to the KMT, Chiang Kai-shek resigned as President of the Republic of China, entrusting power to Li Tsung-jen. The KMT then orchestrated a massive retreat to the south, knowing that the battle for China was lost.

The PLA entering Beijing (Beiping).
https://commons.wikimedia.org/wiki/File:PLA_Enters_Peking.jpg

By the end of April, the People's Liberation Army crossed the Yangzi, taking even more major cities in central and eastern China. Nanjing—the nationalist capital for many years—fell in a matter of days. As the KMT forces garrisoned in these areas surrendered to the Communists, many civilians found the PLA to have also truly liberated them from the terrible regime of Chiang Kai-shek. However, although both sides had been engaged in peace talks and the Communists had basically swept the nationalists throughout the country, the CCP nevertheless continued its march to the south, chasing the KMT all the way to Guangzhou —a city where the nationalist revolutionary movements had originated decades before the civil war. In late summer, the remnants of the nationalist government, Chiang Kai-shek included, started fleeing to the island of Taiwan, proclaiming the city of Taipei as the new capital of the Republic of China. As the Communists closed in, they took everything they could, including food rations, military equipment, and valuables. The KMT had lost the Chinese Civil War to the CCP. By the end of 1949, the PLA had established its presence in all regions of the country, reunifying China after many decades of instability, war, and chaos. Crucially, on October 1, 1949, the triumphant Mao Zedong formally proclaimed the establishment of the People's Republic of China in the reinstated capital city of Beijing (which had been renamed Beiping during two decades of KMT rule). The Communist revolution of China was complete.

Chapter Six – The People's Republic of China

Rebuilding China

It is not easy to imagine the cost of the bloody conflict between the KMT and the CCP, which lasted for nearly two decades (with some breaks). The civil war had been reignited after the Second United Front was dissolved following the events of the Japanese retreat. In only that period, the People's Liberation Army suffered an estimated 1.5 million casualties to the nationalists' 600,000 (about three times this number likely defected to the Communists). More than six million KMT fighters also directly surrendered or were taken prisoner by the CCP. The civil war is also believed to have had a horrible toll on the civilian population. Over five million people died as a direct consequence of fighting or famine and disease, which spread throughout the conflict. Thus, with the final Communist victory and the fleeing of what was left of the KMT to Taiwan, Mao Zedong and his party had a monumental task ahead of them: not only to rebuild the war-torn country basically from scratch but also to ensure that the path to development followed Communist principles and practices—something that seemed more challenging to the CCP.

The Communist Party's approach to the situation in the early years was rather pragmatic, and historians have remarked that this was largely a wise decision. The CCP did not have nearly enough supporters or personnel to carry out its long-term goal, which was the Communist transformation of the country. The main problem the CCP encountered was a lack of administration and the ability to efficiently govern the areas it had taken over from the KMT. China was a huge country, and establishing a cohesive governing apparatus proved extremely difficult. Although KMT forces were out of the country and the CCP was in control of mainland China, there was still a long way to this control amounting to real power. So, the pragmatic approach meant that the party had to recruit thousands of bureaucrats in different provinces just to keep things running—even though their political orientation might not have been exactly Communist. Technically, many new recruits, occupying jobs of varying importance, were not as avid adherents of Communism as the CCP would have liked, but they were enough to get the job done, whatever the job was: tax collection, infrastructure maintenance, court affairs, etc.

Next to the lack of an effective connection with the central government, the main problem the CCP encountered in the countryside was the locals' keenness toward the traditional social system, which gave rise to new barriers among different peasant classes. When it came to agricultural collectivization, the CCP had some experience, but pushing for land reform on a much larger scale proved much more difficult. The CCP's intention was to not only redistribute the land equally among the rich and the poor but also root out the influence of the rich landlords, upon which the whole traditional system was based. To achieve this goal, they did not rely on locally-recruited bureaucrats unfamiliar with the Communist cause. Instead, Beijing regularly sent traveling work groups that supervised the collectivization of land and resources. These work teams traveled from village to village and ensured the process went as smoothly as possible, although never quite forcing the rich to radically give up all their lands. Together with local bodies of government, they increased the taxes on the rich, canceled some debts of the poorer peasants, and reduced the overall rent the poor paid to the rich.

These measures did not outright strip the rich of all their power but provided a basis for the Communists to operate in the future and for the common people to see firsthand the merits of

Communism. The party had correctly realized that pushing for a complete equalization of wealth in the rural countryside was basically political suicide. The rich were influential in the eyes of the poor, so if the CCP did not at first demonstrate that their proposed system could work, no one would support it. Compared to other Communist regimes that targeted the rich elite in one organized sweep, as in Vietnam in the mid-1950s, the Chinese approach was slower and more methodical, resulting in the local peasants trusting the new government. In the end, the early land reform of the People's Republic of China contributed massively to the national economy, eliminating landlords who had wrongfully utilized their power and influence and gaining much trust and loyalty from the lower-class peasants.

It would be the early 1950s before the economic reforms severely affected the state of things in more urban areas, touching capitalistic private owners and companies in different fields of commerce and production. The CCP's goal always was to have a planned economy, but this required the transition of property and businesses from private to state ownership, and, in a country as large and disorganized as China, the process was complicated. So, just like in more agrarian parts of the country, the Communist Party's approach to the urban economy was gradual at first. The CCP wanted to maintain the rate of production and services that existed in the cities, especially since (as we will cover below) the country was at war in Korea against the United Nations (UN) forces. Pushing for the abolition of classes outright required cohesion and economic power that simply did not yet exist in China.

In the opening stages, the CCP mainly targeted private business owners, often referred to as "bureaucratic capitalists." This group consisted of people affiliated with the previous KMT government, who became the subjects of a quick and violent CCP crackdown. In addition to the already state-owned industries, businesses held by the bureaucratic capitalists were taken over at once. By 1951, key industries, such as transportation and heavy industry, were almost completely controlled by the state. From 1952 onward, the government introduced the "Five-Anti" Campaign, directed against the rest of the bourgeoisie. Its main objective was to address problems of bribery, tax evasion, dishonest labor, or any possible economic criminal offenses traditionally associated with the bourgeois class. Of course, it comes as no surprise that the crackdown led to more consolidation of the government's power over the country's economy.

Socialist Transition

From 1953 onward, economic modernization and heavy industrial development took off in China. By then, four years in complete control of the country had given the CCP enough time to mobilize its governing apparatus and establish firm control over all aspects of Chinese political, social, and economic life. The party leaders thus saw fit to proceed with a transition to socialism, which, in their eyes, would bring nothing but prosperity and freedom to the Chinese people. Modeled after the Soviet-style First Five-Year Plan, the CCP embarked on an ambitious journey to transform the country's economy, forcing more collectivization of land in the countryside and taking over more industries and commercial businesses in the cities. The CCP almost completely copied the political and economic institutions and their design from the Soviet Union. The Soviets appreciated this and provided plenty of material assistance for the smooth implementation of a socialist system.

The main goal of the economic changes adopted by the CCP was to develop heavy industry as quickly as possible, most likely because it was a guarantor of the reliable production of arms in times of war. This had been exactly what Soviet Russia had done in the years before World War II, enabling the country to have at least some fighting capabilities after its disastrous defeat in the First World War. Most government investment was directed towards developing highly industrial sectors, mostly in urban areas. But agriculture and other lighter industrial sectors were not nearly as neglected as in the case of the USSR. With help from Russian specialists, many existing problems were addressed, contributing to the economy's growth during this period. In 1955, the government started setting yearly investment, production, and profit goals. Large enterprises experienced great growth rates from 1953 to 1957 (partially because they were easier to keep track of than their smaller counterparts). Investment in industry also led to the spread of technological innovation. For the first time, China started producing modern goods that were in high demand in the global economy, such as machinery and aircraft, moving away from complete reliance on agriculture.

The transition to socialism was much more effective in the industrial sector, while the agrarian sector, the true pillar of the Chinese economy, was not as easily controlled. Yes, the push to move away from dependency on agriculture had been made, and somewhat successfully, but most of the country's population still lived in rural areas, meaning that many of the industrial changes had never quite affected them. The socialist reorganization that had taken place in the countryside—a change modeled after the collective *kolkhoz* farm of the Soviet Union—had envisioned the coming together of several families into cooperative groups that worked each other's lands, though each family still retained ownership of their plots of land. When working, the agrarian families would keep score of who had done what work, and the harvest would be redistributed among the families based on their share. The cooperatives ranged in shape, form, and size, some uniting over 100 families in a village.

It's not hard to imagine many of the problems encountered during this transition, the most prominent of which was the distribution of responsibilities among so many people. In a small family of four or five people, everyone knew what to do with their tools and how to work each plot of land. In a cooperative commune of a hundred families, however, this resulted in the shirking of responsibility, a lack of motivation, technical problems, and so on. Some Communists recognized that there was more potential to increase agricultural production, but this required a coherent and working industry. Adopting a different approach was thus necessary for the country, but what this approach exactly was remained clear.

Early Foreign Policy, the Hundred Flowers, and Mao

Due to the economic measures taken by the CCP, China basically experienced the classic effects of the industrial revolution about one hundred years later than many of its European counterparts. For the first time in a while, people started flocking into urban areas, preferring to work in state-held factories than in agrarian cooperatives, which many of them outright escaped. Population growth was also quite significant, once again affirming that peace and stability were by-products of industrial development and modernization. These two developments, however, resulted in worker-related problems that had first produced socialist and Communist initiatives in Europe in the 19th century: cities were starting to become overpopulated, and factories had no more room for employees or the means to produce enough to keep up with the demand. This, paired with less Soviet assistance than in the first few years of the CCP's victory, posed quite a few challenges for the party. It seemed as if simultaneous industrialization, modernization, and a Communist transformation of the country were proving impossible. A lack of funds and expertise confronted the CCP, which had relied on their Soviet friends for advice and resources in the past.

In the mid-1950s, the CCP also became more authoritarian, establishing an ambiguous and somewhat hostile relationship with many members of the Chinese intelligentsia—people who did not come from backgrounds that would render them part of the bourgeoisie but who nevertheless had enough education to be interested in Western studies. Although the CCP claimed to encourage freedom of speech, expression, and information exchange, the intelligentsia proved to be the main obstacle to widespread ideological reform—an essential part of the Communist system. Interestingly, Mao believed that freedom of speech was important since the educated would not only criticize Communist bureaucrats on the more corrupt side but also fervently support Marxist principles, realizing its complete superiority towards other ideologies of the West. Famously, with the slogan "Let a hundred flowers bloom, a hundred schools of thought contend," a reference to the Hundred Schools of the Zhou period, the Party displayed its wish to encourage free speech.

However, the intelligentsia's response came as a shock to Mao and the CCP. The educated people criticized not only the corrupt bureaucrats of the CCP but the CCP and the Communist regime itself, believing they had the freedom to express their thoughts. This criticism of the system was not tolerated, and weeks after the intelligentsia's response, Mao ordered a complete crackdown on everyone who had dared to speak out against the CCP's rule. The Anti-Rightist Campaign arrested and exiled thousands of critics, as well as thousands of ordinary people who were in some way associated with them. This resulted in an almost complete cleanse of outspoken anti-CCP persons from urban areas. To this day, many believe that the Hundred Flowers was nothing but Mao's bait from the beginning, his lie to draw out potential opposition to the party in true totalitarian fashion. In any case, the crackdown on the anti-Communist intelligentsia went a long way when toward ideological revolution.

Mao Zedong, Chairman of the CCP, ca. 1959.
https://commons.wikimedia.org/wiki/File:Mao_Zedong_in_1959_(cropped).jpg

The final aspect of the People's Republic of China we should mention before returning to the economic policies of the late 1950s is the country's international position and foreign policy after the Communist victory. The post-war era drastically affected the policies of the CCP and its standing on the international stage, especially since the Cold War between the United States and the Soviet Union was just taking off when the Communists gained power in China. The Chinese position was clear from the very beginning: in 1950, they signed a treaty of friendship and alliance with the Soviets and became a very important part of the Communist sphere. China was not as strong as the Soviet Union, but it nevertheless had lots of unexplored potential. The fact that the Americans had let the CCP take power in a country that could have been so influential in global politics in the coming decades was certainly a defeat for the Americans, who had only engaged with the CCP as part of their efforts to drive out the Japanese.

The first clear point of conflict between the Chinese and the West came during the Korean War of 1950-1953. The Western forces under the UN banner, led by the American General Douglas MacArthur, launched a counterattack in support of the democratic South Korean government, which was being invaded by the Communist North. (The country had been divided into two camps post-war.) MacArthur's forces saw much success, outmaneuvering and outfighting the Soviet-supported North and heavily pushing them back. China had not been involved in the Korean War at this point, but the American (UN) advances made the Chinese wary of a potential capitalistic occupation of Korea—since Japan had used the peninsula to launch its invasion of China in the past. Thus, the Chinese cautioned the Americans to refrain from pushing further to the Chinese-Korean border in the North. The CCP even sent a few thousand Chinese troops into Korea to fight against the Americans so that they would reconsider the push and agree to a ceasefire, but to no avail. Thus, when the Chinese Army crossed the Yalu River in October 1950 to resist the UN's advances, the overly-confident American soldiers were surprised, forced to retreat and give up their positions. Eventually, after two more years of back-and-forth, the two sides agreed to a peace deal that is still in effect today—a Korea divided into a Communist North and a democratic South.

The Korean War turned out to be a defining point in Chinese foreign policy. It basically shaped the hostile relationship between Beijing and Washington, DC, that would persist for decades and result in the United States' decision to back the exiled KMT government in Taiwan.

Chiang Kai-shek and his supporters, who had managed to flee from Mao and the CCP, had organized themselves somewhat comfortably on the island, claiming to be the legitimate government of China, although the CCP controlled more than 98 percent of the country's population and 99 percent of its total land area. In reality, in the early years after its exile, Chiang Kai-shek had only managed to survive because the CCP did not have the means to cross the 110 miles of ocean and launch a naval invasion. The KMT was armed to the teeth, yes, but the sheer power of the Communists would have been more than enough to take the island. Still, before the Korean War, the US had never considered Chiang Kai-shek and the exiled nationalist government a useful ally.

After the Chinese involvement in the Korean War, however, the US proclaimed that it once again allied itself with Taiwan and would protect the island against any Chinese effort to go to war. This was a crucial development, still in effect today, that resulted in the prosperity of Taiwan thanks to gracious aid from the United States. The Taiwanese economy flourished, setting an example for other countries in the region. Washington also refused to recognize the CCP government for many years, referring to Beijing by the old name of Beiping and utilizing its influence over other countries to do the same. The US not only denied the CCP government diplomatic relations but also, until 1971, denied it UN membership. The US also forbade American citizens from buying goods from China and regulated its exports. In short, for many years after the establishment of the People's Republic of China, relations with the United States, the leader of the free capitalistic world and the most powerful country at that time, were more than strained. The situation is much better today, but the US is still the biggest ally and supporter of Taiwan and the exiled nationalist government.

The Great Leap Forward

In 1958, under the leadership of Mao, the CCP adopted its most influential and ambitious policy program—a change that would bring immense social, economic, and political consequences to the Chinese nation. The infamous Great Leap Forward was an incentive proposed by Mao and his supporters that sought to increase agricultural production since the planned economy had failed to produce a large enough surplus to complement the levels of industrial growth from 1953-1957. The government, putting faith in people, wanted to reorganize the rural population and workforce to reach this goal: to push for a communist society in its true form, in which the labor done by the people would not be the marker of what they would receive and everyone would work out of sheer goodwill and enthusiasm because that was what was right for society.

Let's briefly look at the Great Leap Forward, an ambitious but ultimately failed implementation of the principle "from each according to his ability to each according to his needs," which would forever alter the CCP's approach to governing the country.

It must be mentioned that the political climate that influenced Mao's decision to push for such a radical reorganization of rural labor came partially from the newly-born tensions between Beijing and Moscow after the death of Joseph Stalin and the assumption of power by Nikita Khrushchev as the new First Secretary of the Soviet Communist Party. With the announced policy of de-Stalinization, Khrushchev wanted to diverge from the traditional approach to the Soviet model in which Stalin had occupied a central role for multiple decades. Mao, on the other hand, believed that the move would bring nothing but negative consequences to world Communism and began to question the Soviet model as a whole, driving a wedge in Sino-Soviet relations that would only widen as time passed.

Mao had always closely surveyed Chinese rural life and had placed utmost importance on peasants when it came to revolution in China. He thought that developing the agricultural sphere was as conducive to a successful revolution in his country as industrialization. Mao's initiative to transform and boost the agricultural output of China thus stemmed from a divergence in thought from the Soviet model, which took the products generated by agriculture and channeled them to serve industrial and urban development. In August of 1957, during an assembly of China's Central Committee, Mao announced the creation of "people's communes," which were huge agglomerations of rural families into economic and social groups on a scale never seen before. About 26,000 of such communes were organized throughout the countryside, with each containing an average of 5,000 households.

People's Commune canteen.

To boost large-scale activities in the communes that benefitted overall production, the CCP established boarding schools for children so that their parents had more time to work, shared dining halls so that fewer people had to spend time preparing food, and larger fields (by combining smaller, individually-held plots of land) so that more people could work on them more efficiently. With everyone working long hours in almost extreme conditions, the CCP expected the agricultural output of 1958 to double that of 1957, which would have been a total economic miracle and one of the most successful models ever implemented in the world. With a load of propaganda and political messages accompanying the announcement, the Great Leap Forward launched in February of 1958, envisioning a complete transformation of China's agricultural life for the next five years.

The first eight months of 1958 saw amazing results, surprising many doubters of the initiative, even inside the party. Reported numbers of agricultural gains were soaring much higher than in previous years thanks to great weather, which contributed to the success of the large-scale communes. Such reorganization of labor also made it possible for peasants to get involved in industrial production, not just agriculture. Many peasants were simply not needed to work the shared plots of land, so they instead began setting up small industries, most importantly the "backyard steel mills" (or "backyard furnaces"), which were capable of producing tons of low-quality steel and would dramatically increase its production in the country. Some peasants also began setting up uranium mines after being taught how to spot uranium deposits on the surface, which greatly boosted China's uranium production and allowed the country to develop its first atomic weapon (which was perfectly good, unlike the steel). With such high gains in agriculture, as well as in industry, the CCP was more than satisfied and began demanding greater results for 1959, intending to dwarf the achievements of the program so far. To achieve this, they reorganized the labor force even more, pushing more people into the industrial sector from agriculture.

This was when the situation began to worsen for the Great Leap Forward. Scared of not meeting the goals set by their superiors, low-level bureaucrats in charge of monitoring the production of their communes began reporting inflated numbers, which were, in turn, wrongfully used for planning by the CCP—to the detriment of the overall situation. This led to the CCP's higher and higher expectations, causing a chain reaction of false reporting and more demand that spiraled the communes' hard-earned success into complete disarray.

For example, the numbers were so exaggerated that some communes began offering more generous meals to thousands of peasant families (which was obviously a mistake because they couldn't afford to), leading to the depletion of most of their food reserves over the winter-spring period of 1958-1959. This was just one of the problems. Bad weather and over-exhaustion from work led to a smaller harvest in 1959 than in 1958, resulting in widespread hunger that affected urban areas as much as the rural countryside. To put things into perspective, it's estimated that more than 9,600,000 people died in 1959 alone, about 1.45 percent of the population and the highest death rate the country had experienced in years. 1960 was no better, and the death toll, added to the already-existing array of problems of the Great Leap, resulting in 26 percent less agricultural output than in 1957 and a staggering 17 million deaths. These numbers finally caused the CCP to abandon the Great Leap Forward by the beginning of 1961. The situation partially improved, but it would take several more years before China could return to the state of things before the policies of 1958. Although the official numbers are disputed, it is estimated that no less than 30 million people died as a direct result of Mao's policies from 1959-1961. The Great Leap Forward is still considered one of the worst tragedies of the 20th century.

Reaction to the Great Leap Forward

By 1961, when the Great Leap Forward was recalled by the CCP due to the atrocious results it had produced, members of the governing party realized they needed to make several policy changes to backtrack on some of the problems caused by the latest endeavor. By January 1962, a very interesting development marked this change of attitude: Mao, although still retaining his position as party chairman of the CCP, stepped down from being the chief administrator of the day-to-day policies in the country, giving the role to Liu Shaoqi—the new chairman of the People's Republic of China since 1959. Shaoqi, alongside several prominent Communists from the party, including Deng Xiaoping, led the efforts to bring China out of the political and economic crisis created by the Great Leap Forward. Mao's importance was not diminished; however, the fact that his proposed policy had been a failure forced the dictator to wisely retreat and observe how his fellows would run the country.

Under Liu Shaoqi, the PRC tried to backtrack on some of the changes introduced in 1958, most importantly the people's communes. For example, it reduced the size of families inside the communes. Smaller communes meant that the work done by individual peasants would be easier to track, and the merits could be more evenly distributed. Not only that, but in some areas of the country, the communes were almost totally dissolved, with the party returning to the redistribution of peasant-owned lands along the lines of the original land reform. More private ownership was thus encouraged—a radical diversion from the policies of the Great Leap. These changes were followed by a return of thousands of Chinese to the countryside from the big cities, as the party had declared that overpopulation in the urban areas had become a problem. The economic freedoms given back to the peasants in the rural areas also contributed to this shift.

Workers in the cities, on the other hand, were not lucky enough to gain such economic freedoms, and their jobs were still decided by the government apparatus: the government assigned jobs, usually for life, to city workers, but it also provided higher job security and decent pay, enough for everyone to live normal lives. These changes were also a part of a bigger policy of population control. In a big and underdeveloped country such as China, keeping track of population was relatively difficult, especially considering the horrors of the Great Leap Forward. With the reorganization of communes, the return of people to the countryside, job assignment, and a newly-implemented system of residence permits, however, the CCP made a great effort to monitor its population. To ensure that large-scale reorganization of the communes would be difficult in the future, the residence permits made it difficult for peasants, for example, to enter and live inside the cities or cross regional boundaries and start working in other provinces. Following these policies, economic goals were also made more modest and realistic, as opposed to the ambitious demands during 1958-1961.

The policies of Liu Shaoqi and Deng Xiaoping proved very successful in the first few months after their implementation, massively improving the detrimental economic and social climate left after the Great Leap. However, the emergence of more moderate leaders in the CCP, such as Liu and Deng, alongside Mao's retreat to the relative background, eventually caused differences in the direction of the revolution. China was not a fully Communist country, and the recent defeats of the CCP had signaled exactly that. Economic stability and high levels of industrialization were needed for a successful revolution, but Mao and many high-ranking officials of the party also emphasized the ideological side of the revolution. Mao thought that the traditional elements of the revolution—the class struggle upheld by most of the population, including workers and peasants in the case of China— were being forgotten. These had been the main reasons behind the Sino-Soviet split after Khrushchev's de-Stalinization policies, which Mao extensively critiqued throughout his time in office. Mao did not like a revisionist approach to the revolution, believing that it failed to grasp its essence, which was the will and enthusiasm of the proletariat to overcome the bourgeoisie. For these reasons, after being in the background of CCP policy-making for quite some time, Mao decided to return to the foreground once again and redirect the revolution in a more favorable direction.

The more pragmatic method of economic and political reorganization adopted by Liu and Deng, which built on the already somewhat pragmatic model of revolution implemented by Mao himself, was, in fact, working. The country was seeing quite a bit of progress from the tough period of the late 1950s, but Mao's insistence on returning to the premier political scene changed the situation. Throughout 1961-1965, when Liu's and Deng's reforms were still being implemented, Mao actively campaigned for domestic and foreign policy initiatives that would complement his more utopian view of the revolution. One of the most important of these was his proposal to reform the education system, in which family background played a major role in developing a student's career. For example, students would get assigned special class labels based on the occupations of their parents and their relationship with the CCP, and admission to good schools would be based mostly on such labels instead of the competence of the student. This meant that even after the Communist takeover, China had failed to completely escape from traditional, Confucian-like systems that favored elitism and status. To circumvent this and many other similar problems that clashed with the utopian communist view Mao adhered to so much, Mao and his supporters needed to implement a good propaganda model to convince the masses.

A solution in this regard would come in the form of the army—an institution that would be used by Mao as a model for ideal discipline and uniformity. Lin Biao, the commander of the armed forces and Mao's fervent supporter, certainly contributed a lot to this idea, and so did the military developments of the early 1960s. In October 1962, China briefly became involved in a war with India over a border dispute—a conflict in which the Chinese PLA assumed a swift victory over the Indian forces and pushed relatively deep into the Indian territories before deciding to retreat and organize a demilitarized zone in the disputed area. The success of the military further pushed the prospect of an ideal Chinese Communist citizen, adding to it the most important elements of a soldier—discipline and obedience. Mao and Lin Biao considered the army an ideal model for what the revolution aimed to achieve from its citizens. Then, after reorganizing the army's internal bureaucratic structure, Mao insisted that many administrative institutions also borrow from the army, increasing its emphasis on the day-to-day affairs of regular Chinese life. Coupled with an extremely effective propaganda campaign to promote the army, its main principles as ideals for the civilians to strive for, and its heroes as heroes of the people, the PLA's importance greatly increased.

Domestic propaganda of Mao's vision for the revolution was coupled with China's newly-assumed role on the international stage, which diverted once again from the traditional Soviet approach. For instance, the country engaged in diplomatic relations with many of the young African nations, as well as traditional partners of the US, like France. In addition, tensions with Moscow continued as Mao blamed the Soviet Union for not standing up to the imperialist United States during the Cuban Missile Crisis of 1962 and called out Khrushchev for his reluctance to aid China in the border dispute with India. These led to the development of a more nationalistic spirit inside the country, further amplified by the increased importance of the PLA as the institution that embodied the nationalist spirit the best.

The Great Proletarian Cultural Revolution

Years of successful propaganda from Mao and his expressed desire to get back to the very top of the party (although he had never truly left) to purify the intents of the revolution once again eventually materialized in the Great Proletarian Cultural Revolution, launched in May of 1966. The tense domestic political climate that preceded the Cultural Revolution was clear among the members of the CCP, who felt the tensions between the reformist Liu and Deng on one side and Mao and his supporters on the other. What many historians believe triggered Mao to incentivize the Cultural Revolution was the deputy mayor of Beijing, Wu Han, an academic who had joined the CCP after the civil war and had recently written a fictional play about a virtuous state official who was dismissed from office by an idiotic emperor. Mao took the contents of the play as criticism towards him, as the plot closely resembled his actions when he had dismissed the former army commander Peng Dehuai from office in 1959, accusing him of being a representative of an anti-CCP faction. Mao denounced Wu Han and his play soon after its publication in late 1965 and traveled to Shanghai, where his base of support was the highest.

Mao's chief aim appears to have been to reduce the power of the ruling elite of China. In this goal, his main supporters came not from the Red Army but from the country's young student body. Propagandizing that he wished to finally purge the remaining bourgeois elements from Chinese culture and create a new educational system that valued true Communist ideals, Mao's message resonated highly with the students, who were further motivated by special work groups sent by Mao to different schools and towns. At first, it seemed as if everything was going to play out as it had during the Anti-Rightist Campaign of 1957, but the movement soon escalated on a different level. In May of 1966, Beijing University students started putting posters on walls, promoting the Cultural Revolution and advocating for it to become a nationwide movement of great importance. This instance was documented and reprinted in national newspapers by order of Mao, leading more people to pay attention to the students, who had started organizing themselves into the "Red Guards." The Red Guards verbally attacked professors and members of the administration in their universities and schools, accusing them of being from bourgeois backgrounds and basically anti-Communist.

The students claimed that they were primarily against the "Four Olds": old ideas, old culture, old customs, and old habits. These had polluted the social lives of Chinese people and clashed with more noble Communist principles advocated for by Mao and the true Communists of the CCP. In addition, the students began criticizing things that had nothing to do with traditional Chinese society—namely, Western culture and its influences, including capitalism. Destroying anything that remotely resembled the Four Olds or the evil imperialist West, the Red Guards also started to abuse the owners of such materials. In a few weeks, word started to spread that the students had become increasingly violent, even beating people they accused of being bourgeois to death on several instances.

These demonstrations continued for nearly two months. Then, in early August of 1966, Mao issued a statement by the name of "Bombard the Headquarters," which severely altered the direction of the movement and gave it a whole new purpose. In his statement, Mao claimed that destructive, reactionary bourgeois elements existed even inside the CCP and motivated people to attack such officials. Soon, it became clear that Mao's targets were the more moderate reformers of the previous few years—Liu Shaoqi, chief of state of the PRC, and Deng Xiaoping, the CCP's general secretary. In September, at a rally that would be attended by hundreds of thousands of Red Guards, Mao encouraged the revolutionaries to work towards rooting out such corruption and bourgeois elements from the CCP, leading to the attack and arrest of many individuals associated with Liu and Deng. Now, they were the main enemies of the Cultural Revolution.

A Maoist propaganda poster from the Cultural Revolution.
https://commons.wikimedia.org/wiki/File:Mao-era_Propaganda_Poster_Featuring_Chinese_Typist.jpg

In the following months, the movement gained more and more supporters. Millions of people joined the Red Guards, traveling around the country to personally see historically important Communist sites, like Mao's birthplace or the city of Guangzhou. New groups, comprised of industrial workers, started forming as well, complementing the Red Guards and emerging as powerful forces in the Cultural Revolution. Their aim was the same, and they were also motivated by Mao's propaganda of the true Communist cause and the rooting out of the bourgeois elements from the CCP.

"To rebel is justified" was the motto of Mao during these months, encouraging more and more people to join the movement, which was slowly turning into a personal war against the "bad" Communists.

During the Cultural Revolution, Mao would almost attain the status of a god, enjoying widespread support and devotion among the revolutionaries as the man responsible for modern and prosperous China. He was adored by the Red Guards, and his writings became very sacred among the revolutionaries. The students would religiously carry and read a small copy of *Quotations from Chairman Mao,* the "Little Red Book," a collection of Mao's past writings. He was the center of the Cultural Revolution and enjoyed emperor-like popularity among the masses, especially throughout 1966, elevating his status inside the party and in foreign countries. The idea of the revolution soon became two-fold: that the common people were virtuous and brave enough to be the catalysts of the revolution and run the society themselves without bourgeois domination, and that to achieve this goal, Mao's guidance was the only way.

Red Guards in 1966, holding Mao's *Quotations.*
https://commons.wikimedia.org/wiki/File:Red_Guards_in_Tian%27anmen_Square.jpg

In 1967, the Cultural Revolution entered yet another stage, with Mao encouraging revolutionary groups to enter and seize government offices and buildings. This call radicalized the movement beyond recovery and led to the escalation of a chaotic situation. As more and more revolutionary groups joined the movement, their intentions and aims became increasingly ambiguous, especially as the CCP appeared fractured from within. The most radical members were Mao supporters; then came the less radical group (mostly military high command) with Lin Biao as its head and the moderate wing still trying to operate the government under Premier Zhou Enlai. The revolutionary groups were backed by these different CCP factions and accepted varying initiatives from each of them. The chaos eventually spread to almost all provinces of the country, and violent clashes with groups of conflicting interests resulted in thousands of deaths and horrible behavior. This part of the Cultural Revolution is stained with accounts of ritualistic, ceremonial cannibalism, in which some radical Red Guard members would cook and feast on the bodies of their defeated enemies just to send a message. The atrocities that showed themselves during this period clearly demonstrate the violent and radical nature of the Cultural Revolution—a movement that had started as a protest of the old-fashioned elements of Chinese culture and turned into something much worse.

By 1968, the army was heavily involved in the revolution, but its main goal was no longer to aid the Red Guards in terrorizing the anti-Communist officials and members of the public. Instead, the army would be used to discourage the revolutionaries from such violent actions. Mao even agreed in late July to work with the moderates to put an end to the chaos. The independent power of the Red Guards was undermined by the army, acting on behalf of the government, and led to the transportation of millions of Red Guards from cities to the countryside, putting an end to the violent demonstrations in the urban areas. The Red Guards were reorganized to work the land with the peasants, which stabilized the situation a bit. Mao declared the Cultural Revolution over in 1969, and the CCP issued a new constitution that praised Mao Zedong and gave him a central stage in the guidance of the People's Republic of China. But the second phase of the revolution would soon erupt again and last until 1976, after which more purging would end the radical movement.

Power Struggles of the Early 1970s

The immediate results of the first stage of the Cultural Revolution affected millions of Chinese, especially in urban areas, since that was where the movement had been concentrated. The initial goals of the movement, by 1970, produced changes in the country's educational system meant to root out the leftover bourgeois-elitist elements in the schools. The role of examinations—a big part of the traditional Chinese schooling system—was significantly reduced. Many more students had the chance to get admitted to the country's universities, which before had sorted out admission largely based on the social status of the students' parents. In addition, many public officials and members of the intelligentsia now had to attend the "May Seventh Cadre Schools"— rural establishments where they had to relocate, live, pursue agricultural lives, and get reeducated with Maoist principles. Changes were also made to the health system to make public health more accessible to the rural population. In short, while some of the initial intentions of the Cultural Revolution were addressed, the new implementations were essentially further propagandistic tools of the central government to ideologically reform its subjects. The chaos and suffering created by the movement were still largely ongoing in various parts of the country, although not to the same extent as in the early days.

More importantly, the early 1970s was a period of political maneuvering among the country's highest-ranking officials. Mao still stood at the very top of the country and the CCP, but his more ambiguous role over the past few years had raised a lot of questions about party leadership and succession. Lin Biao had always been considered a potential successor of Mao and had previously been praised for his close relationship with the dictator, but some of his latest remarks during the central committee meetings had not been as friendly towards Mao as Mao would have liked, perhaps.

Meanwhile, as the relationship between Mao and Lin slowly deteriorated behind the scenes, China secretly received a historic diplomatic visit from Henry Kissinger, representing US President Richard Nixon. The 1971 visit between Kissinger and Zhou Enlai turned out to be monumental for Chinese foreign relations.

Eventually, it led to a visit from Nixon himself—a diplomatic move from Washington that sought to capitalize on the Sino-Soviet split and establish formal relations with the PRC to gain a potential upper hand in the Cold War. Nixon, in a way, considered the Soviet Union a mutual threat to the US and China. His initiative to normalize relations with the Chinese came as a shock to most of the world. Eventually, this would result in the PRC's official recognition by the UN as the main representative of China —taking the distinction away from the exiled government in Taiwan.

Henry Kissinger (left) meeting with Zhou Enlai (center) and Mao Zedong (right).
https://commons.wikimedia.org/wiki/File:Kissinger_Mao.jpg

After the death of Lin Biao in September of 1971 in a plane crash, an event that followed the successes of Zhou on the foreign policy front, the balance of power between the highest-ranking officials of the CCP began to swing in favor of Zhou. Mao and the party's ruling elite deemed the fatal plane crash Biao's effort to escape to the Soviet Union, leading to the purge of his supporters in military and public offices, especially when officials discovered conspiratorial plans by Lin's son directed against the government. Zhou thus briefly enjoyed the status of Mao's successor until he was diagnosed with a fatal cancer. This development followed the worsened health of Mao himself, who suffered a stroke in 1972. All of this further elevated the importance of finding the country's future leaders. Still, Zhou Enlai was a lovable character for the masses, something that played a big role after his eventual death.

Thus, in a surprising move, Mao and Zhou, both old, dying men, decided to back Deng Xiaoping as the successor of party leadership. However, since Deng had been a moderate ex-reformer purged by Mao and the Cultural Revolution in previous years, the more radical wing of the CCP protested his return to mainstream politics. The leaders of the radical wing, the "Gang of Four" that included Mao's wife Jiang Qing, Wang Hongwen, Zhang Chunqiao, and Yao Wenyuan, had risen to prominence during the early stages of the Cultural Revolution and were instrumental in the radicalization of the movement and the purge of more moderate/right-leaning officials of the CCP. From 1972 onward, after a moderate Deng had been reinstated to a powerful position within the party, the Gang of Four tried gaining Mao's favor to undermine Deng's return. Eventually, Deng would take over many of Zhou's roles and initiatives after the latter fell ill in mid-1974. He would push for the implementation of a reform program called the Four Modernizations, aiming to improve Chinese agriculture, industry, technology, and defense. As a moderate, he would help some of the important officials who had been the targets of the radicals during the Cultural Revolution, and his vision for the future would be heavily contested by the Gang of Four.

The radical Gang of Four gained the upper hand over Mao by 1976 as the more moderate wing of the party, led by Deng, was starting to gain more prevalence. The radicals viewed Deng and his supporters as innate enemies of the revolution, claiming they were bourgeois rightists who wished to undermine the merits of the Cultural Revolution and Maoism in general. The ailing Mao seemed to have fallen under their influence on his deathbed in 1976, leading to him criticizing the policies implemented by Deng during his time in power. Then, in January of 1976, when Zhou Enlai passed away, Deng delivered a sentimental eulogy speech at his funeral, remembering him as the hero of the revolution and the Chinese people who had brought prosperity and popularity to the country—a message which deeply resonated with the people. To see how the situation would unfold after the death of his greatest ally in the CCP, Deng fled to Guangzhou. His wariness about the ill intentions of Mao and the radicals came true: his policies and initiatives were formally denounced by the party leadership in the spring, and it seemed that the radicals had finally gained the upper hand. As Deng saw his supporters purged by the radicals, the future of the country and the party was still in the air.

Chapter Seven – Modern China

The Death of Mao Zedong

Chairman Mao passed away on September 9, 1976, at 82. His death would mark a new era for the People's Republic of China—a period of initial political instability and uncertainty followed by great change and economic revival, eventually leading to the country's transformation into a superpower. As the country entered a week of official mourning, there were still many things to be decided regarding party leadership and the direction of the CCP, which basically had been run solely by Mao for the past few decades. It would not be one of the Gang of Four or Deng Xiaoping who would come to dominate the CCP after the death of Mao, however. Instead, it was a member of the Politburo Standing Committee, former Vice Premier and Minister of Public Security Hua Guofeng, who would emerge as Mao's successor. Having been one of Mao's personal favorites, Hua had accumulated significant prestige inside the party but retained a low-key image compared to Deng or other possible replacements for Mao. With this prestige and support from some of the key party members, which mainly stemmed from Hua's avid advocacy of Mao's policies and approaches, Hua maneuvered his way to the top, becoming the new chairman of the CCP.

It is this period following Mao's death that is often recognized as the real end of the Cultural Revolution. Most historians agree that the movement's impact was monumental even though it hardly reached most of the population throughout the years. The Cultural Revolution had mainly succeeded in forming a cult-like image of Mao and Maoism while failing to achieve significant social or economic results. It also affected the CCP and its image, which was heavily damaged during the early 1970s, with the Red Guards often violently demonstrating against the CCP officials and storming and damaging their offices. The differences between party members were also forged during this period. But, with Hua's accession to power, he would quickly balance the existing disagreements within the party due to the movement, mainly the radical-moderate split that was more-or-less normalized within the CCP from 1977 onward. At the 11th National Congress of the Chinese Communist Party in mid-1977, Deng Xiaoping and his supporters were reinstated, and the purge would officially end. Moreover, Hua reduced the influence of the Gang of Four, instead pushing for the "Two Whatevers" policy—an approach to politics guided by "whatever instructions Chairman Mao gave and whatever policy decisions Chairman Mao made."

Economic Revival

Surprisingly, although many believed that the Chinese system might collapse after the death of Mao, the opposite became true. From the late 1970s, the country experienced a miraculous, nonstop rate of economic development, a massive improvement from the stagnating years of the 1960s and the early 1970s. The government pushed for economic revival policies with the Four Modernizations adopted as the main program and Deng Xiaoping as the initiative's foremost advocate. A large amount of government investment started flowing into trying to get the domestic economy running again, which had largely become inactive and frail due to the years of political turmoil in the country. The importance of the agricultural sector was highlighted once again, and changes were applied to the commune system to gradually disband the entire system. Step by step, peasants and peasant families were offered opportunities to exit their communes, with agriculture becoming increasingly private and individuals responsible for less communal lands than after the radical land reforms. This, paired with more freedoms around crop production and even the restored option to move around, significantly increased agricultural output in the following years. In the early 1980s, excellent weather also helped accelerate the results of these changes.

Deng Xiaoping during his visit to Washington, DC
https://commons.wikimedia.org/wiki/File:Deng_Xiaoping_at_the_arrival_ceremony_for_the_Vice_Premier_of_China_(cropped).jpg

In addition to this, a crucial development took place in the late 1970s that helped China get its economy up and running again—the formalization of diplomatic relations with the US in 1978, followed by new diplomatic ties with the rest of the world and the eventual opening of the country's economy to foreign trade. The country started attracting foreign capital and businesses, which dramatically transformed its economic situation, leading to a boom in the urban areas. The establishment of Special Economic Zones (SEZ) in the big cities resulted in urban development on a large scale and helped accelerate China's strive towards the Four Modernizations. International investments flowed into Chinese cities with long-lasting, generational impacts. Material incentives were proposed to overcome some of the innate problems with the relative liberalization of the urban economic space, including difficulties in price allocation and the struggle for influence between the government and the new businesses.

This economic development was supplemented by the nationwide encouragement of the young population, which also led to an educational boom. New universities, especially in technical and scientific fields, popped up all around the country as domestic and foreign investments provided much-needed funding. Students were also encouraged to study abroad, with thousands traveling to the West to gain higher education. Eventually, China reached a point where it was (and remains) a unique hybrid: a largely authoritarian Communist state that allows a large degree of economic freedom and privatization—inherently opposing principles.

Domestic and Foreign Policy

Although China today remains a largely undemocratic, one-party state, that is not to say that, since the death of Mao, significant political developments have not shaped the country's approach to domestic and foreign policy initiatives. As we have already mentioned, in the late 1970s, political freedoms were largely reinstated to many formerly-purged officials, Deng included, and these politicians would lead the way to reform and change. Post-Cultural Revolution, many members of society also found much-needed relief, as the discrimination and crackdown that had been a staple of the country during the movement finally stopped, giving many people previously nonexistent career opportunities. By the early 1980s, Deng and the more moderate coalition of Chinese politicians had essentially been the leaders of the CCP's policies and shaped much of the political processes inside the country. In 1981, Chairman Hua was succeeded by one of Deng's closest allies—Hu Yaobang—a man who only occupied the position of chairman of the CCP for a year before the title was officially dissolved. From 1982 onward, he continued being the CCP's general secretary, essentially having the same powers and privileges as the chairman.

After Yaobang's succession as chairman, the party underwent several major reorganizational changes in which many bureaucratic offices were outright abolished or significantly restructured, cracking down on in-party corruption and ideological differences between the party's Maoist and the reformist leaders. As the transitory period after Mao's death ended in 1985, the country had to confront major social and political challenges caused by the fast-paced implementation of many changes during the previous years. These changes had brought many benefits to the country as a whole but had also impacted the general worldview of its citizens—especially the youth, who had finally been exposed to Western standards of living and ideas. These young people, deemed "bourgeois liberals" by the more radical members of the CCP who wanted to crack down on the demonstrators, took to the streets in the late 1980s to demand more personal freedoms and overall liberalization.

With the death of Hu Yaobang in 1989, who had been considered one of the main advocates for more liberalization of the Chinese political and social sphere, hundreds of thousands of protesters, mostly young students, took to the streets in major Chinese cities. Ambiguity inside the party, as well as between Communism and the newly-implemented freer economy, produced mass unrest for several consecutive weeks starting in April 1989. The clearest example of this was the one million demonstrators assembled at Beijing's Tiananmen Square, who coincidentally got a lot of worldwide media coverage since their protests coincided with the visit of the USSR's Mikhail Gorbachev to Beijing. There was great debate as to how the protesters should be dealt with, with Zhao Ziyang, the new moderate general secretary, advocating to grant them more freedoms and concessions. Still, in the end, the party's radical wing had the final say, insisting on a forceful crackdown and suppression of the protesters. In early June, in an incident that came to be known as the Tiananmen Square Massacre, the CCP ordered the military to violently deal with the gathered protesters, opening fire on the peaceful demonstrators. By June 5, as the military cracked down on the activists in other big cities, the CCP managed to completely restore control, causing the deaths of at least several thousand people.[2]

The Tiananmen Square Massacre was followed by very important changes inside the CCP, as well as in its approach to the country's domestic policy. Jiang Zemin replaced Zhao Ziyang in 1989 as the new general secretary, and under his leadership, the party tried to restrict the public political sphere and reestablish a firmer hold on society. By the early 2000s, the government had adopted a more conservative approach, especially compared to the liberal policies after Mao's death. The economic system remained largely capitalistic, with numerous private enterprises in the Chinese market, but the CCP's hold over these businesses was tightened because of the mass unrest that had followed economic liberalization. At the same time, the country's international status continued to rise, leading to more normalized relations with the outside world, including prestigious permanent membership status at the UN's Security Council. The reforms under Jiang Zemin and later Hu Jintao—president of the PRC until 2012—led to even more development of the Chinese economy. It eventually became the second-largest economy in the world in the 21st century—set to overtake even the US.

---

[2] It would be good here if you can find the famous Tank Man photo. I wasn't able to get my hands on a royalty free version of it.
https://upload.wikimedia.org/wikipedia/en/d/dd/Tank_Man_%28Tiananmen_S quare_protester%29.jpg

Conclusion

Civilization in China has existed for thousands of years—one of the first in the world. Its ever-changing history is extremely interesting to observe, as the socio-political processes for thousands of years have eventually led to our understanding of modern China today. Still, despite many influential periods in the country's history that are vital to painting an overall image of China, perhaps none are quite as important as the last 150 years, which saw a complete transformation of the country, including the abandonment of traditions and practices that had been around for several millennia. Modern China is an intriguing case of how the drive for ideological and social change and modernity can impact the lives of millions of people, something which was especially highlighted by the end of the 19th century.

Modern China continues to enjoy its recently-gained role as an internationally dominant country, with vast material and human resources that dominate many fields of life throughout the world. This position owes almost everything to intellectual developments that originated in the country in the late 1800s, a period that found the Chinese empire divided, on the brink of collapse, and unable to stand up to outside intruders. As the vilification of the Chinese people continued in the 20th century, new forces led the way to change and revolution, attempting to construct a modern society that they believed most resembled humanity's constant historical tendency towards change.

Marxist doctrine, in a way, appears to be both the salvation and curse of the Chinese people. Yes, it was crucial to the industrial and social development that enabled the country to catch up to its competitors. On the other hand, Chinese Communism also led to the deaths of tens of millions of people, who were essentially stepping stones for totalitarian leaders to push for a radical transformation of China in hopes of achieving a utopian society. Mao Zedong, the central figure in modern Chinese history, is not remembered in history books as a great reformer who led the country's struggle against foreign imperialists of Japan. Instead, he is remembered as one of the most brutal dictators of the 20th century—a time that is otherwise full of blood-hungry dictators. Mao is one of the best examples of how totalitarianism, justified by a blind ideological drive towards utopia, can lead to catastrophic results for the people it is imposed upon.

Although modern China has largely moved on from the country's destructive 20th-century policies and has become a political and economic powerhouse, it still largely fails to emerge on the world stage as a prosperous, democratic nation that upholds liberal values. The utopian Communist society for which the country's leaders had strived for more than 100 years has not yet been achieved. In fact, under the leadership of current President Xi Jinping, China has become even more totalitarian in recent years. As globalization and information exchange become more and more prominent, the country has been associated with numerous human rights violations, including heavy labor camps against ethnic minorities in Tibet and Central Asia, illegal organ trafficking, and increasingly anti-democratic practices against its people. The Communist Revolution in China never had these goals in mind when it originated in the 1920s, but it can largely be blamed for these malpractices that are the country's black spots in an otherwise rich and compelling history.

Nevertheless, it is not only interesting to observe future developments in modern China but also important for all of us, as the country has managed to occupy a tremendous role in each of our lives, moving from the depths of isolation and traditionalism to the changes that took place in its recent history.

Here's another book by Captivating History that you might like

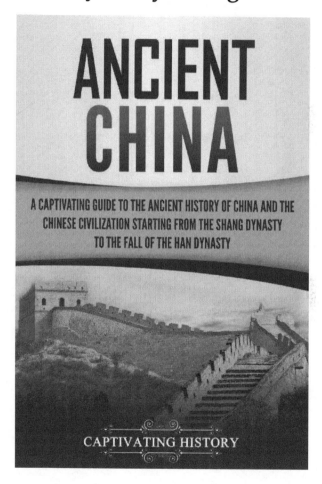

Free Bonus from Captivating History (Available for a Limited time)

Hi History Lovers!

Now you have a chance to join our exclusive history list so you can get your first history ebook for free as well as discounts and a potential to get more history books for free! Simply visit the link below to join.

Captivatinghistory.com/ebook

Also, make sure to follow us on Facebook, Twitter and Youtube by searching for Captivating History.

Sources

1. Dittmer, L. (1980). "The Legacy of Mao Zedong." *Asian Survey*, *20*(5), 552–573. https://doi.org/10.2307/2643907

2. Dittmer, L. (2017). "Taiwan and the Waning Dream of Reunification." In L. Dittmer (Ed.), *Taiwan and China: Fitful Embrace* (1st ed., pp. 283–300). University of California Press. http://www.jstor.org/stable/10.1525/j.ctt1w76wpm.18

3. Fenby, J. (2008). *Modern China: The Fall and Rise of a Great Power, 1850 to the Present* (First U.S.). Ecco.

4. Kayloe, T. (2017). *The Unfinished Revolution: Sun Yat-sen and the Struggle for Modern China.* Marshall Cavendish Editions.

5. Lee, H. Y. (2020). "The Politics of the Chinese Cultural Revolution." In *The Politics of the Chinese Cultural Revolution.* University of California Press.

6. Li, W., & Yang, D. T. (2005). "The Great Leap Forward: Anatomy of a Central Planning Disaster." *Journal of Political Economy*, *113*(4), 840–877. https://doi.org/10.1086/430804

7. Li, X. (2015). *Modern China (Ser. Understanding Modern Nations).* ABC-CLIO.

8. MacFarquhar, R., Royal Institute of International Affairs, & Columbia University. East Asian Institute. (1974). "The Origins of the Cultural Revolution (Ser. Studies of the East Asian Institute)." Published for the Royal Institute of International Affairs, the East Asian Institute of Columbia University, and the Research Institute on Communist Affairs of Columbia University by Columbia University Press.

9. Mao, Z. (1990). *Quotations from Chairman Mao Tsetung.* China Books.

10. MITTER, R., & MOORE, A. W. (2011). "China in World War II, 1937–1945: Experience, Memory, and Legacy." *Modern Asian Studies, 45*(2), 225–240. http://www.jstor.org/stable/25835677

11. Ng-Quinn, M. (1982). "Deng Xiaoping's Political Reform and Political Order." *Asian Survey, 22*(12), 1187–1205. https://doi.org/10.2307/2644047

12. Peng, X. (1987). "Demographic Consequences of the Great Leap Forward in China's Provinces." *Population and Development Review, 13*(4), 639–670. https://doi.org/10.2307/1973026

13. Taylor, J. (2009). *The Generalissimo: Chiang Kai-shek and the Struggle for Modern China.* Harvard University Press.

Made in the USA
Monee, IL
07 July 2024